The Sporting Fords
Vol 3: CAPRIS

The Sporting Fords
Vol 3: CAPRIS

A collector's guide
by Jeremy Walton

MOTOR RACING PUBLICATIONS LTD
Unit 6, The Pilton Estate, 46 Pitlake, Croydon CR0 3RY, England

ISBN 0 947981 45 4
First published 1983
Second Edition 1990

Printed in Great Britain by The Amadeus Press Limited,
Huddersfield, West Yorkshire, HD2 1YJ

Contents

Introduction

Since 1969, the Capri in many of its production and competition guises has provided me with some memorable moments as well as enjoyable and (usually) reliable transport. In 1981, I was pleased to recall such experiences and to provide an immense amount of competition data of specialist appeal in my book *Capri: The Development & Competition History of Ford's European GT Car* (GT Foulis). Now, in producing a *Collector's Guide* to the more sporting models which appeared during almost 18 years of Capri production, I have been faced with a rather different task.

This time the objective has been to marshal the facts of Capri production and model details in a more orderly manner than was originally possible. The fact that Capri production finally ceased in December of 1986 has allowed us to revise this second edition thoroughly with the benefit of hindsight. I have also been able to pay more attention to numbers produced, and in which period. I feel that the German production record is particularly interesting in this respect as by far the majority of all Capris were made under the aegis of Ford of Germany, who were solely responsible for production from October 1976 until the end of the run. In Britain we made just under 340,000 of the total of 1.89 million Capris manufactured between 1968 and 1986.

Competition and the likely pleasures of ownership, including a sharp look at the problems of secondhand purchase, are included in this new work, emphasizing the pleasurable side of the Capri's character that was such an important ingredient of the original design.

I feel that the Capri's combination of distinctive appearance (especially in the 1969 series), cheap parts of good availability, and mechanically straightforward character will turn the higher-performance derivatives, particularly of the now obsolete 3-litre V6, into appreciating as well as enjoyable collector's cars. There will always be some who decry the Capri concept as producing a car of fashion rather than function. Yet these critics should remember that a combination of above-average aerodynamics and effective engineering kept this Ford right up to scratch in motorsports against the best that BMW and others could pit against it in the production classes. The Capri's racing record in the more radically modified classes (or its achievements during a period as a four-wheel-drive rallycross competitor more than a decade before the Audi Quattro) show a basic worth beyond mere fashion.

Above all, the Capri was built to provide the ordinary motorist with a touch of glamour and enjoyable driving at an affordable price. Today it is easier than ever to own such a car — but how long will it be after production ceased before the ravages of time reduce the desirable Capri population sharply? I hope this *Collector's Guide* will not only facilitate your search for a reasonably priced modern classic, but will also enhance your interest in, and appreciation of, the most individualistic of European Fords.

JEREMY WALTON

Acknowledgements

Of course my main debt regarding the provision of information for this book must be to the members of Ford Motor Company in Britain and Germany, who bore with this third bout of Capri interrogation by me so stoically. Martyn Watkins, on the Public Affairs staff in Britain, offered his usual patient wisdom in either supplying or pointing me in the right direction for many of the figures used, but I have also had the benefit of other Ford departments whose staff do not wish to share the limelight. In some cases Ford decline to supply production/sales figures to the press, either because to do so would benefit their competitors, or because of the complexities involved with competition recognition.

The assistance and information on practical matters I received from many Capri owners and Ford dealerships was considerable. This edition owes particular thanks to Dennis Sellars, Capri RS3100 concours specialist and parts professional at Quicks of Manchester. Steve Saxty, former Tickford Capri owner and keen Capri Club International member, added especially to my 1989 insight into suspension and gearbox variations.

Updating the Zakspeed Capri story was carried out with the help of author and then Ford Motorsport Director Karl Ludvigsen, at Ford of Europe. Many of my former colleagues at Ford Advanced Vehicle Operations and Ford Motorsport personnel at Boreham provided further information regarding Ford policy on the RS2600 and RS3100 derivatives and the four-wheel-drive Capris.

Pictorially much of the material has come through Ford Photographic, at South Ockendon, a department managed as cheerfully as ever by Steve Clark, who knows he couldn't do without Sheila Knapman's sterling work, either!

Editorially, my working years for *Motoring News*, *Motor Sport* and *Cars and Car Conversions* have been most important to me, but I also had vital help from *Autocar* (who were a tower of strength in providing me with so much of their very accurate road-test data at such short notice), as well as *Classic and Sportscar*, *Autosport*, *Motor* and a number of German magazines, including *auto motor und sport*. Also, although at times we seem to agree to disagree, I should like to acknowledge that I would not be writing books at all had it not been for the constant encouragement and practical advice provided by Graham Robson, whose many worthy motoring books include the first two volumes of these *Collector's Guides* devoted to the *Sporting Fords* — those concerned with the *Cortinas* and the *Escorts*.

JEREMY WALTON

The 1961 Classic was a development of the 105E Anglia theme, and while its style may have been too American for many European tastes, its 1,340cc engine, disc front brakes and quadruple headlamps were useful features upon which to build the first Capris.

The Capri name was first used for this coupe version of the Classic, introduced in 1962 and sharing the 54bhp three-bearing 1,340cc engine.

CHAPTER 1

Ancestors and parentage

The Mustang and Cortina influence

On April 17, 1964, an estimated 29 million television viewers in America were faced with the bright and breezy commercials that marked the official launch of the Ford Mustang. Some 2,600 newspapers carried the message that the Mustang, essentially a car with more exciting convertible or hardtop bodywork over well proven saloon car underpinnings, was available at prices from $2,368 (£846 at the prevalent exchange rate). Urged on by displays at 100 Holiday Inns and 15 major airport terminal buildings, the public practically fought to own this affordable new status symbol from Ford. Even in the early-1980s, nearly 20 years after the Mustang's phenomenally successful announcement (some 100,000 were sold in the first four months), Lee Iacocca is best remembered as the Ford General Manager in his thirties who spawned the Mustang, rather than the Chrysler Chief Executive in his fifties.

It took only two years for Mustang sales to reach a million units, an unheard of record for a speciality car of any kind, never mind one with such sporting pretensions. *Life* magazine called it 'a sports car for the masses', and it forced Ford's domestic market rivals into a market that was quickly dubbed as one for 'Ponycars' in honour of the Mustang name.

The Mustang itself could almost be all things to all men (and an increasing number of women drivers, so accurately identified as wanting more than just a family barge). Within the framework of a two-door body every aspect of the car could be tailored to the customer's wealth and inclinations. Over the years the Mustang badge was to be attached to convertible, hardtop, notchback and full fastback bodies covering engines from the puniest four-cylinders (although originally a 101bhp straight-six was the minimum equipment) to what was generally regarded as an underestimated 335bhp of the limited-production 7-litre V8s.

Although one could argue that the Mustang only had a sporty appearance over rather soft saloon car running gear in its original form, there was no reason to cast aspersions on its racing potential when Shelby American Inc, of Los Angeles, sold 562 of their modified Mustang GT-350 models to the public and race-prepared a further 12 GT-350Rs. Available from late-1965 onwards at prices which started at double that of the original models, the Shelby Mustangs were an integral part of Ford's competition image and the cornerstone on which the Mustang's competition potential was explored. In later years the Shelby label would be debased severely on cars which were merely jazzy alternatives made in Dearborn, but by the late-1960s Ford had their own Boss 302 5-litre pumping out 290bhp in basic trim and accompanied by all the suspension and braking features that were needed to secure the premier American TransAm Championship title against opposition that included teams run by Roger Penske, Dan Gurney and Jim Hall's legendary Chaparral business.

Thus the concept of a two-door car that was visually exciting to carefully assessed cross-sections of the public, and which had the basic design versatility and simplicity to accommodate the widest possible range of engines, was proven on the world's largest car market. Although Ford would often protest that the Capri was no 'European Mustang', their own company personnel frequently referred to it as such . . . and the first styling studies for Capri were coded Colt, a veritable son for Mustang! Ironically, the Europeans did not take to the Mustang in significant numbers, nor did Ford seek to sell it as anything more than a limited

The first Capri GT was the final evolution of the Classic-Capri low-production run, ceasing production in Summer 1964. Its 1.5-litre, five-bearing motor was shared with Cortina and Corsair GT variants and developed 78bhp.

availability special option for a few Europeans who wanted something different, but the Capri name was to invade the American market in its hundreds of thousands. Such was its success that many Mustangs, those sold by the Lincoln Mercury Division, were badged as Capris after American sales of the European car ceased. Then, after this period of use on both road and racing Mercuries, the Capri name was considered evocative enough to be revived in 1989 for an Australian-built front-drive sports car aimed principally at the USA market.

European background

Ford actually offered a Capri in Britain years before the Mustang went on sale. Owing its roots to the debut in July 1961 of the Ford Classic 109E, the 117E Capri was made between July 1962 and July 1964 and was offered in two forms — a standard model with a 1,498cc four-cylinder engine developing 59.5bhp and later a GT model with a 78bhp version of the same power unit. The 11,143 Classics built in 1961-62 were equipped with a 1,340cc engine producing 54bhp.

Manufacture of the Capri GT derivative did not begin until February 1963 and ceased in July 1964, by which time 5,101 complete ordinary Capris and 470 Knock Down (KD) kits had been made. The GT production figure for the original Capri was 1,767 complete cars and 235 in KD components, making a grand total of 7,573 Ford cars carrying the Capri label even before approval had been given for basic styling studies of what we best know today as a Capri.

Both the Classic and the Capri bore heavy American influence in their styling and they made little pretence at sporting handling, although both models did have disc front brakes as production fitments, which was certainly not the industry norm for Britain in 1961. Contemporary road tests reflected a general disappointment with the Classic, upon which theme the Capri amounted to a larger-engined hardtop coupe successor. Add in the very low production figures and there's a strong temptation to dismiss the Classic/Capri foray as an over-publicized failure in the pre-Cortina era. However, this seductive theory is discounted by company historians, who point out that the tooling for the Classic/Capri series was upon soft-metal dies that could only have

been intended for limited output over a comparatively short period. Apparently we should regard the Classic/Capri as a temporary holding series while the 1962 Cortina was being readied, a model that did not reach full output until the following year.

Planned failure or otherwise, those first Capris gave Ford of Britain a chance to assess public feeling towards the type of personal coupe that had proved so popular in the United States when Ford launched the Thunderbird in 1956.

Early in 1965 Ford of America gave the go-ahead for styling studies for the car which would make its debut as a Capri in 1969. Despite the sales success of the Mustang, Ford executives in Britain, where all work on the project began under that Colt coding, felt that they must justify their reasons for marketing such a speciality car. By the time the Capri went on sale, much of their logic also had to be applied to the European market, for in June 1967 Henry Ford 2 had approved the formation of Ford of Europe.

Ford of Britain's internal marketing memos cited the late-1950s as the beginning of the reasoning behind the Capri concept. In

Major inspiration for the Capri project came from the success in the USA of the Mustang, first of the 'ponycars'. This is the GT 2+2 fastback version; the car also came as a convertible or a 'notchback' hardtop, and with a whole range of different engines and equipment options. Styling ideas for the Capri showed Mustang influence from the outset, though the dummy side vents were one of the few elements to remain recognizably present right through into production.

1959 both the BMC Mini and the Ford Anglia had taken motoring to an even wider audience. One Ford executive told me, 'these cars enabled millions of motorists in the early-1960s to throw off the shackles of public transport'. Then Ford studies revealed that disposable income had increased to twice that of 10 years before. More interesting still for a company wanting to sell a car that was more than basic transport was the fact that freshly affluent Britons increased their car expenditure by a staggering 197 per cent during 1957-65! By 1965 the British were buying a million new cars a year for the first time, and still more important to the Capri's future was the way in which customers were lapping up ever more expensive versions of basic models. This had started with the De Luxe and Super approach, featuring badgework to impress the neighbours, and at this point Ford started to make use of their transatlantic sales flair, but in a European context, and in 1963 they introduced the Cortina GT. The GT suffix was to become *de rigeur* for any sporting saloon right through to the 1970s, by which time Ford would be responding to the extra cash in the consumer's pocket with the aid of E, S, GLS and Ghia badges, all providing significant specification improvements over the more basic versions of the same car.

Cortina basics

Before the first drawings and styling exercises of 1965, the company used the closing months of 1964 to lay down the design brief for the Colt project. The marketing department's first priority was that the car be 'extremely good looking'. Next came a requirement that four or five people with their luggage be accommodated, but the British engineers always regarded this with faint amusement and the original Capris appeared with the back seating carefully moulded to hold two. The Mustang concept of a long bonnet and short boot also meant that rear legroom was bound to be restricted and luggage space limited compared with a saloon of equivalent wheelbase.

Other basic requirements listed in that 1964 briefing included a need for a full utilization of existing engines and a wide variety of optional trim. Lower down the briefing came 'exceptional ride, handling and control with a very low noise level', and 'available at a family budget price'.

Although the styling studios had a brief which amounted to

providing a new body that would draw new Ford customers into the showrooms (in America half of the Mustang's customers traded-in non-Ford products), the engineers faced the task of saving as much money as possible by using current production parts beneath the anticipated 'body beautiful'.

In fact the first prototypes, run under the direction of Ford engineer John Hitchman in order to assess the Capri concept in action, were Cortinas, their spring rates, damping and suspension geometry set to accommodate a car that would be heavier, lower, wider and longer than Ford's favourite saloon, despite a shared wheelbase of fractionally under 101 inches. To disguise the first running prototype in 1966 they taped up an apparent four-door 'glassback' body and discovered that the low ride height provided the best handling motor car on crossply tyres these engineers had yet produced.

While the mechanical components were tested in their new home, which would carry on the Ford of Britain suspension tradition of a leaf-sprung rear axle and MacPherson-strut front layout, the styling side raised some fundamental headaches. Styling outlines from America, Germany, Britain and possibly from the Ford of America-blessed studio in Turin that had provided the Mustang concept, all attempted to define a shape which would force the public either to add a second car to their family, or to deliberately ignore practicalities like accommodation in the face of emphasized style.

Ford assessed public reaction to some of these styling dreams as well as the glass-fibre full-size models dubbed GEX and Flowline, using customer reaction shows in London, Brussels, Geneva, Hamburg, Milan and Amsterdam to explore the feelings of potential buyers — who were not aware of the identity of the host company. By June 1966 American Ford of Britain Chief Executive Stan Gillen had all the favourable answers required to authorize a complete development and production programme based around a clay model created in America. The estimated cost of turning the Colt project into reality was £20 million, a fleabite compared with the £500 million which Ford were to record as the cost for creating the new Escort CVH engine roughly a decade later!

Although the GEX full-size styling studies were very close — particularly in side view — to the final product, there were features that the public reacted against most strongly in Europe.

One of the earliest serious Capri studies was signed by Rossi and dated November 17, 1965. Note that the 'hockey-stick' body crease is present as well as retractable headlamps, a feature used by the late-1960s Mustang derivative, Lincoln Mercury division's Cougar.

Principally the objection centred upon a feeling of claustrophobia experienced by people who tried the rear seating with its minimal side glass. Such a window layout had its origins in the very successful Mustang hardtop – as opposed to fastback – models, and it was with great reluctance that the stylists increased the rear side window area and also made the line from the rear roof to the wing panels one continuous flow instead of the favoured separation which had provided a distinct demarcation between the passenger and luggage accommodation in the case of the Mustang.

But the larger U-shaped rear side window found favour with the public at subsequent consumer clinics and so that shape was officially adopted. By then it was known that the Colt name could not be introduced to the motoring public on the flanks of the new Ford coupe as it was already registered in Japan. Today we know it as the marketing identity of the giant Mitsubishi Corporation for cars sold on the British market, including a number of coupes... By November 1967 Ford had approved the name Capri. As in the case of the Escort announced in 1968, this was a revival of an earlier but short-lived nameplate.

Mechanical progress

The birth of Ford of Europe during the summer of 1967 extended the mechanical development of the Capri from its British concept to that of a vehicle which would be manufactured in both Britain and Germany. That year Ford had opened a new body and chassis engineering centre at Merkenich, where it was readily accessible from Ford of Germany's headquarters in Cologne, Northern Germany. The Merkenich engineering centre had its counterpart amongst the landscaped acres of Dunton, where Ford of Britain's research centre was also opened in 1967 with its emphasis on engine development and including a small banked figure-of-eight test track and, subsequently, full emission test facilities.

As Ford went European, so did the Capri. When the British began Capri development they merely knew that it would be required to handle both in-line and V-pattern four-cylinder engines of anything between 50 and 102bhp. For German manufacture there would be a completely different range of engines, all of them V-pattern, but including V4s and V6s; late in the British development programme (1968) it was decided that

Styling studies from the 1960s reveal the gradual evolution of the Capri design. The main sketch (original signed simply 'Birtley') clearly forecasts the eventual frontal appearance, with Escort-style rectangular headlamps, but some of the others have more of a show car character. The intention to introduce elements of the Mustang's style is clear in the mock side air intakes, lower right.

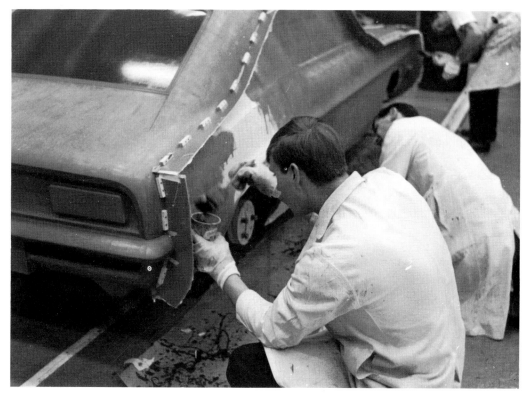

Modelling up a full-size glass-fibre Capri for management appraisal in March 1966. We can see that the key elements such as the body crease and general appearance had been forecast, but the choices had to remain open as long as possible for a car that would sell largely on its styling.

the UK range would also be headed by a V6, in this case the Heron-headed 3-litre as fitted to the Zephyr/Zodiac saloons. In both Britain and Germany the most powerful versions of the Capri, with their extra fuel tankage, reinforced bodywork and, in the case of the British V6, an engine thoroughly re-engineered around the bottom-end to cope with oil surge and high temperatures under duress, went into production nearly a year after the original Capri.

The British in-line fours owed ancestry to the 1968 Ford Escort and to the version of the Cortina Mark 2 introduced the previous September. Available in two stages of tune (GT designating the higher output in the market place), both engines belonged to the 'Kent' family and displaced either 1,298 or 1,599cc. Shared

design features included disposition of exhaust and intake on opposite sides of the cylinder head — dubbed by Ford as 'crossflow' — five main bearings for the crankshaft and a block-mounted camshaft to drive overhead valves that sat in a cylinder head which had a virtually flat face. Combustion chambers were built into the pistons on the Heron principle.

The British V4 and V6 units also utilized this Heron head layout and shared both bore and stroke, the six displacing 2,994cc and the four 1,996cc. The V4 had first displayed Ford's interest in Heron heads with its debut in September 1965 in the Corsair cousin to the Cortina.

Because the decision to insert the V6 motor was not taken until 1968, Ford's Public Affairs department recoursed to the rather

Two pictures of the full size Capri model made for assessment in 1966. The Corsair badge is of course just a red herring, but the 'GEX' lettering on the rear quarter panel prefigures the XLR nomenclature used later for option packs. Most of this model's primary styling points did reach production, with the notable exception of the very small rear side window. Note the beam front axle to make the model mobile, and what look like Zodiac Mk 4 wheel trims introducing a strong element of Americana.

Ford kept struggling away with the side window design as late as 1968, by which time this prototype displayed production hubcaps, mirrors and another attempt at the 'air intakes'.

clever ploy of creating extra interest in a performance Capri by asking the Boreham-based competitions department to convert eight 1968-built Capri 1600GTs with the Ford Cosworth BDA engine of 16-valve, double-overhead-camshaft cylinder head construction. These cars did not go through any development at Dunton, but they did serve to show the press a tougher side to the Capri before the more powerful models could be made available; even the V4 was not sold until several months after the public launch in 1969.

Meanwhile, the Ford of Germany units that could be fitted beneath that long bonnet were all 60-degree V-formation units, but that was really the only common ground they had with their British contemporaries. All the German engines were interrelated and made maximum use of common bore and stroke combinations. For example, the 1,288cc, 50bhp motor that began the range had an 84mm bore, as did the 1,999cc units of 85 or 90bhp, but the latter were V6s instead of V4s. The 1,288 and

1,488cc German V4s shared the same 58.86mm stroke while the two V6s offered at the initial launch (of 1,999 and 2,294cc) utilized the same 60.14mm stroke. Completing the juggling act, the German motors of 1,488, 1,688 and 2,294cc all had the same bore size.

Transmissions, too, were those of existing Ford products on either side of the Channel. In Germany, they rationalized the gear ratios to the point where all models shared the same gear sets, any tailoring to suit the engine and body weight being arrived at through a variety of final-drive ratios. In Britain, two sets of ratios were specified, the two larger-engined Capri GTs sharing gearboxes of Cortina GT/Corsair 2000E ancestry, while the plain 1300 and 1600, plus the 1300GT, suffered a wider set of ratios. All models, British or German, shared the single-rail gear selection system which had already provided such a high standard of change in the new Escorts. These general comments cover the Capris sold from the February 1969 launch date; the later and

Another 1968 prototype, F-plated and apparently ready to go, complete with petrol stains from the high-mounted fuel filler which is now located on the opposite side. Four Ford adults within are trying desperately to decide if that rear side window really is too small to offer the public. Criticism at the fashionable 'customer clinics' centred on the claustrophobic feelings of anyone trying the rear seat accommodation.

This model dating from late November 1968 retains the garish wheel trims, which were thankfully not to feature in the final specification, but displays the enlarged, U-shaped side window eventually adopted in response to further market research. Close inspection reveals the old, abbreviated style still fitted on the far side.

Escort and Capri together in the course of development and testing carried out in Africa by engineers from Ford Cologne. The LHD Capri now has the final rear side window shape and the padded three-spoke steering wheel of the production models.

more powerful V6s were a different matter and required a separate development programme with associated heavy-duty components.

Development details

Supervizing the practical progress of Capri engineering was Jim Moncrieff, whose 10 prototypes amassed a lot more European mileage than would have been usual in pre-Ford of Europe days. The Lommel test track, with its simulated Belgian *pavé*, and real Belgian road surfaces were used in a maximum effort to provide some semblance of passenger comfort (particularly in the back) with the limited suspension movement which could be provided. It was an integral part of the Capri's character that it should ride as low as possible, and in providing a modest 3½in of movement before the axle hit the bump stop rubbers, the engineers certainly complied with those styling considerations. The rubber-bushed

radius arms that Ford had used for sporting Cortinas appeared for the Capri, but in this application they did as much to limit the travel of the axle as they did towards locating the unit against acceleration and braking tramp. As with the multiple-leaf rear suspension, the coil spring rates used for the front were the stiffest then offered on a production Ford, while Armstrong and Girling both contributed dampers that were biased in favour of sporting handling.

Although it would be many years before companies such as BMW or Alfa Romeo agreed that rack-and-pinion steering was an essential part of a sporting car, for Ford in Britain it was unthinkable to use any other system, even though their experience was confined to the Lotus Cortina and the 1968 Escort. Geared at a little over three turns from lock to lock, it was found that it made the Capri, which was roughly three inches lower than the Cortina, a most satisfying driver's car. On one

19

occasion it was probably too satisfying, when one of the first prototypes was rolled at the test track after its intrepid driver had provoked it into a rather more lurid sideways slide than even his considerable experience could handle!

More serious crash testing of handbuilt Capri prototypes worth in excess of £30,000, as well as Cortinas and Corsairs modified for extermination in the cause of the new Ford coupe's impact resistance, was another aspect of development that most potential buyers probably found a rather boring subject, until they needed such protection! The Capri emerged from these tests with credit, the long nose, the padded and strong steering wheel, plus the exceptional strength of those thick, curved rear pillars proving that a pretty face can also be a friend indeed when the Capri driver is in distress.

There were naturally detail points on which British and German tastes diverged in the way that their coupe should perform. Judging from the way in which Capri suspension spring and damper rates were continually altered over the years, this was one area where no real solution could be found, although the 1970s appearance of gas-filled dampers certainly alleviated the perennial ride question. Another difference of opinion occurred over the remarkably effective Aeroflow ventilation (a leading Cortina feature) which the Germans found could not be prevented from emitting blasts of cold air when heat was not required at autobahn speeds. Under British conditions customers were unlikely to spend a day travelling at 70mph or more, but for Europe this had to be cured.

The Capri delivered from engineering to production in 1968 — in which year only 3,855 examples were to be made, leaving Ford perilously short of stock for post-announcement sales in early-1969 — was unique. That it was imitated so widely is sufficient comment on the balance of style, comfort, cost, reliability and performance that Ford provided. In the 1980s the world turned to the smaller front-drive machines from Japan and from VW, but here again the Ford concept of creating a more alluring coupe style on a proven saloon-car base continued, for what is a Scirocco but a sleeker two-door Golf?

Just how close a relation was the first Capri to the pioneering 1964 Mustang? Was it just a three-quarter-scale model, using a Cortina instead of a Falcon base? Judge for yourself from these facts. First, there was only one Capri body style and that was the fastback, which was not offered until the Mustang was in its second model year, when it supplemented the earlier convertible and notchback bodies. There was considerable Ford interest in a Capri convertible early in the model's life, and Carbodies were commissioned to make an example that was tested by some journalists, but there was never anything like the volume in Europe to justify such a proliferation of bodies as the Mustang could offer. To put that into perspective, 1966 Mustang production comprised 607,568 units (including over 422,000 hardtops) while the Capri's record production year (1970) produced 238,979 cars.

Dimensionally, the original Mustangs and Capris measured up as follows, with Capri figures in brackets: Wheelbase, 108in (100.8in); overall length, 181.6in (169.4in); width, 68.2in (64.8in); height for a fastback Mustang was 51.6in (50.2in for a V6 Capri or 50.7in for less powerful models) while the V8 Mustangs had exactly 3in extra front track over Capri (56in against 53in) and had the same rear track width of 56in, whereas the Capri ran on a narrower rear track of 52in. Powered by the straight-six engine the 1964 Mustang Fastback weighed 2,621lb while the 1969 Ford Capri V6 totalled 2,380lb.

Our homework complete, we can now consider the worthiness of the selection, made in August 1968, of a theme for the Capri advertising campaign that had to translate into an irresistible buying urge in 14 European nations if the newcomer was to be a success. The theme was: 'Capri — the car you always promised yourself'.

The first generation: 1969 to 1974

'The car you always promised yourself'

Some £22 million had been expended by Ford on the Colt-to-Capri programme prior to production beginning at the company's factories in Cologne and Halewood, Liverpool, in November 1968. Understanding that this investment had been made in a coupe that was all about affordable image, Ford's three major advertising agencies and expertly staffed public relations divisions ensured that only those bereft of any media contact could remain in ignorance of the Capri's debut.

The preparation for such a publicity assault was undertaken while Capris were scarce on the 1968 ground and had to cover such diverse needs as straightforward advertising, brochures and acquainting both the press and Ford dealers with the new product at first hand. There were nearly 500 Ford showrooms in Britain and they needed at least one car to show potential clients what all the fuss was about. To generate enthusiasm for the new coupe Ford flew some 2,000 dealer personnel to Malta GC. This massive airlift was split into three main convoys, the dealers landing at the wartime airfield of Ta'Qali, where they caught their first sight of the cars they would have to sell at prices from the £890 7s 10d (£890.39) of the basic 1300. Naturally, every facility was employed to show the cars in the right light, but many of the dealers returned overwhelmed by that skilfully planned relief from Britain's December 1968 weather — and the chance to meet Ford of Britain's Managing Director, Bill Batty. Despite a shortage of cars, the Capri would sell at roughly twice the rate anticipated for Britain.

The press were also flown away in December, 250 of them driving Capris over a revealing test route in Cyprus. The 'red herring' 1600GTs, with their 1,601cc Cosworth BDA engine, glass-fibre bonnet and 6J Tech Del Minilite magnesium-alloy wheels provided many an exciting test drive. Yet 'BDA Capri' was obviously going nowhere with its 120bhp engine somewhat hard-pressed to provide convincing performance in a car that was considerably bulkier than the Escort RS1600 in which this exciting 16-valve unit eventually found a limited production home from January 1970.

Public debut

So far as the European public were concerned, there were a number of occasions on which Capri made its 'first' appearance! January 21, 1969 saw the new Ford unveiled at a Bonn ceremony to celebrate its production in nearby Cologne. January 24, 1969 was the official motor show debut with a last-minute Capri display at the Brussels Show after Ford had overcome internal arguments which centred on the foolishness of displaying a car that was not in adequate supply to service demand. February 5 was the date on which sales commenced across Europe and there can be no doubt that Ford's multi-million pound sales effort had been thoroughly worthwhile, for this speciality car, aided by a late advertising decision to emphasize the family over the sporty side of Capri character, reached a production level of almost 214,000 units in its first year.

A walk around the new Capri in 1969 provided enthusiasts with endless discussion points. Was it just a pretty face for the Cortina? When would they be able to buy an engine to fill that enormous underbonnet area? Would the nose be vulnerable when trying to join suburban traffic streams? One thing was for certain, if you disliked the looks this was one car that could be struck off

After all the styling exercises, models and prototypes, this was the final production form of the 1969 Capri. This 1600GT lacks the matt black paint that disfigured so many of the XLR-pack Capris of the original series. The steel road wheels, though similar in style to those of the Cortina 1600E, were unique to the Capri, and the reduced amount of chrome apparently diminished their appeal to thieves!

your shopping list, for at introduction time, with only the in-line fours available in Britain, there were plenty of ways to go faster in smaller packages, particularly the Escort GT/Twin-Cam range of the previous year, if you were Ford-inclined.

In Britain, the range began with that basic 52bhp crossflow 1300 at £890 7s 10d (£890.39), which did not include any of the generally bizarre option packs that we will discuss after exploring the basic British range. Ford then claimed a 0.41 drag factor for the basic body without frills; since it was also on the narrowest tyres and generally had the least amount of optional equipment, we can assume that this was the best aerodynamic factor offered in

the range. Like all these initial Capris the suspension was set to run in rather nose-high fashion, particularly noticeable on motorways, so it may also be conjectured that the Capri's aerodynamic efficiency on the road bore little resemblance to its wind-tunnel behaviour, being rather more akin to Concorde seeking take-off stance!

Ford claimed an 85mph maximum for their slowest and cheapest offering, but they quoted over 20s as the 0-60mph acceleration time of the 1,940lb coupe. To put this in proper perspective, a Ford Escort 1300 Super, then costing £773, and a Cortina two-door 1300, at £809, were quicker through the gears.

The 1968 press party to Cyprus was a great success using distinctive London-registered Capris which were all swiftly sold afterwards. This GT emphasizes that the original British series did not use the bonnet bulge until the V6 model arrived in September 1969. In Germany, the bulge was used far more widely.

It wasn't all sunshine propaganda in Cyprus in 1968. Here on the uplands a plain 1600 displays the final rear-end style with chrome surround and Escort-style strip rear lamps.

Even the 1600GT engine looked small inside the Capri's capacious front compartment.

The 1300GT model was normally advertised as packing 75bhp at 6,000rpm, but these figures were derived from the SAE method and in subsequent years Ford quoted 64bhp DIN for the same engine with its Weber 32 DFE twin-choke carburettor. Compared with a less powerful 1300, the GT crossflow engine had more efficient exhaust and inlet manifolding, plus a more vigorous camshaft to provide that power bonus. However, both engines needed to be worked hard if they were to provide any kind of sparkle in a Capri. The 1300GT cost just under £1,000 and could be compared on the British market to the MG 1300 at £931 or the £851 of the Escort 1300GT. The Capri 1300GT, costing £985 13s 11d (£985.70) had an official maximum of around 90mph and could be expected to reach 60mph from rest in some 15s. By comparison, both the smaller Escort and the MG mentioned would sprint to 60mph in two or three seconds less and reach nearly 95mph — a feat the Capri 1300GT could

A 1969 Capri GT facia with the efficient aeroflow eyeball clearly visible above the oddly divorced headlamp switch; the rest of the rocker switchgear is to the left of the Escort-type minor instrumentation. The bulb to operate the screenwashers, to be seen to the left of the clutch, was a device which many depressed accidentally when using it as an impromptu footrest during hard cornering!

duplicate but, like the Englishman of legend, it needed time. . . .

No, for interesting Capri motoring in Britain one could only start with the 1600GT at over £1,000. There was the plain 1600 at £936 1s 9d (£936.09) but since that had an engine no more powerful than that of the 1300GT, there was little chance of a sporting driver becoming interested, particularly as it had the wide ratios that used to characterize (and spoil) sporting Fords before the advent of the fabled Cortina GT/Corsair 2000E four-speeder with the chasm 'twixt second and third considerably reduced.

The 1600GT carried such a gearbox and the 88bhp SAE twin-choke-carburated engine for a reasonable £1,041. This took it right into the MGB price league of the time, which at an earlier stage in the 1960s would have made Ford the laughing stock of the car community. However, by 1969 six years had elapsed since the separation of the company's competitions department from the main press fleet, the Escort was beginning to pound the best opposition in world-class rallying into the dust, and the Ford Cosworth DFV and FVA racing engines were well-established winners. True, the company still offered the aircraft-carrier excess of the Zephyr and Zodiac saloons, some of these hapless machines wheezing along with the aid of the V4 that in March

1969 would appear in the Capri 2000GT, but it was obvious that Ford were beginning to mount an assault on British Leyland's traditional market leadership; it was to wrest them the number one sales position in the early-1970s.

The Capri 1600GT could hold its head up in the company of the £1,062 MGB in every respect but pedigree. According to *Motor*, the Ford managed just 100mph, compared with the 106.5 and 107mph of the convertible MGB and fastback MGB GT, respectively, but on acceleration the Ford was at least as quick, while its fuel consumption under hard testing was better, although hardly inspired for a 1.6-litre at 22.2mpg. The latter figure, of course, included all performance testing; in the author's 25,000-mile experience 25-28mpg was more likely in demanding road use.

Inside the GT models, Ford had plumped for the heaviest use of instruments and finishes seen in Britain at the price. The heavily padded three-spoke steering wheel stood before a tachometer with a redline tailored to the engine (5,750rpm for the V6, 6,500rpm in the case of 1300GT) which was matched by a speedometer reading anything up to 120mph. Surrounding these two larger dials, the speedometer with its jumble of kilometre and mph markings in yellow and white, were four minor dials with the same affection for bright colours: voltmeter, oil pressure gauge (the 1600GT engine usually had around 40psi, but there was never any indication on the uncalibrated scale), water temperature gauge (the 1600GT always tended towards the blue — cold — end of the scale), and fuel gauge measuring the contents within the 10.5-Imp gallon/48-litre tank, the latter being mounted upright behind the rear passenger seats and above the axle, where its crash test performance had proved excellent.

The basic Capri shared the wide use of the shiny Capri emblem that has since faded from use and the fake wood facia trim. Basic controls were a line of rocker switches placed vertically to the right of left-hand-drive instrumentation and *vice versa* on UK Capris. One steering column stalk was used to cover headlamp flasher, directional indicators, horn and headlamp dipper switch (floor-mounted dip-switches were not unknown in 1969). While the two slide controls and the two-speed booster fan for the heater were conventional, and part of one of the best heating and ventilating fresh air systems put together by any manufacturer, there was the slight eccentricity of a floor-mounted, bulb-action, pressurized air system for the screen washers. Many were the unfortunate keen Capri drivers who would find themselves busily squirting water upon their screens when actually just searching the floor for additional foot-bracing while enjoying the effective handling to the utmost!

All the Capris were better trimmed than average for the class, primarily making use of heavy grade black plastics for items such as the door and seat facings, although German-manufactured Capris used cloth seating inserts widely from the early days.

March hare

The V4 model for Britain duly arrived in March and cost only £46 more than the 1600GT initially, a reflection of the fact that the 2000GT shared pretty well all its running gear, apart from the engine, with its smaller brother. Ford claimed 110bhp SAE for this revised V4, which was not held in overwhelming respect after its earlier performance in the Corsair; the Transit van, the first true European Ford, also used the V4 and continued to do so until the end of 1977. The compact V4 dated back to the 1963 Corsair, which offered 81bhp from a 1,663cc version or 93bhp from 1,996cc. It was the latter 2-litre unit that was uprated for public announcement in July 1967 at 102bhp DIN. The same specification, with Weber 32 DIF carburettor, revised camshaft offering higher lift and sportier breathing, plus slight amendments to the cylinder head porting, was used within the 2000GT. The result was a respectably quick car, given that the V6 was still five months away from its debut. The in-line fours all shared a 7.5in diameter clutch plate, but the V4 was donated an extra inch, all the diaphragm units being activated by the light, cheap and occasionally fragile cable mechanical system.

The 2000GT could record 105-107mph, depending on whether it had the 3.44:1 axle (installed before October 1970) or the later 3.54:1 ratio. Either way the 13in diameter Rostyle fancy steel wheels which all GT Capris shared with 165-13 radial-ply tyres (Goodyear G800s were the most common) provided a very pleasant 19mph per 1,000rpm in top gear. This meant that the rather woolly V4 took 11s or so to haul the 2000GT to 60mph, but the car would certainly manage 24-25mpg, or some 2mpg less than a 1600GT when driven in a similar manner.

Altogether the 2000GT, rather like the later 2-litre in-line fours of the 2000S and Ghia school, was an underestimated

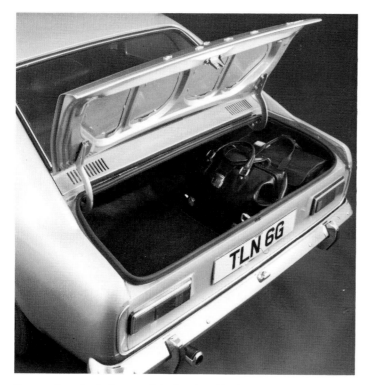

It was not much of a boot, and the later hatchback models were a response to customer criticism on this sore subject, which had revealed the unexpectedly high non-sporting ownership appeal of the Capri.

combination of enough power to make the Capri interesting without the penal insurance rates and heavier fuel thirst of the later V6. However, the engine never had a good service reliability reputation and most of the tuning advice given for the Ford V4 over the years simply amounts to 'don't bother . . .'.

Option packs

If you are confused by car badgework, in recent years the biggest culprits in Britain must be Ford. Besides the GT appellation referring mainly to increased engine power, Ford's marketing department also came up with three option packages

(X, L and R) which could also be combined as XLR to produce the hideous mess of matt black that adorned any GT XLR.

The first X-pack — a name since revived for sporting accessories — cost £32 12s 10d (£32.64) and brought the sort of items that the Japanese forced the Europeans to fit as standard items in later years. The 1969 X-pack consisted of reclining backrests for the seats, individual moulding for two backsides only in the rear, reversing lamps, dipping rear-view mirror, a second interior light, two-tone horns and a handbrake warning light. If one could contain one's natural enthusiasm in the face of such largesse, there was always the L-pack to bring a 'keep-up-with-the-Jones' plethora of Americana like dummy air scoops, bright-finish wheel trims, bumper overriders and enough shiny badges and miscellaneous bits and bobs to keep the neighbourhood jackdaw ecstatic. At £15 0s 4d (£15.02) it was not

The rear seats were plushly trimmed in later versions, such as this 1970 3000E.

The September 1969 Capri 3000GT began a tradition that was to run until 1982 for good-value performance motoring from Capri 3-litre models. The original car cost comfortably under £1,500 in basic trim, but this is the more lavishly decorated XLR version — which showed Ford how keen their Capri customers were to spend more money and thus indirectly led to later E, GXL and Ghia models being produced.

exorbitant, but there were cheaper ways of buying the useful locking petrol cap which formed the practical part of the pack. You could combine X and L packs for £44.7s 10d (£44.39) extra, saving something over £3 by the bulk purchase.

The R-pack was a common item in Germany on its own, but for the British market it was applied to GT models only and was usually combined with the XL equipment for a total XLR price of £79 12s 10d (£79.64). On its own, the R-pack brought 5in wide rims for the standard steel 13in diameter wheels, which had the distinctive spoke pattern that had been popularized earlier on the Cortina 1600E, although the Capri wheels were not nearly so desirable to car thieves, being considerably less shiny, a half-inch narrower and generally less glamorous than the generic term Rostyle (a GKN trademark) had come to imply. Also within the R-selection of goodies were the 15in sports steering wheel with three spokes, modest auxiliary lamps intended to provide extra

range over the equally modest standard headlamps, and a map-reading lamp on a stalk — a nostalgic reminder of the flexible lamps made popular in rallying; purchased on its own, the R-pack was intended to sell for £39 3s 4d (£39.17). A few customers deleted the matt black paint for bonnet, rear boot panel and lower door sills that identified this option and other Fords of sporting inclination, including the Cortina GT and Escort GT.

The V6 in Britain

In September 1969 the UK received what was to be the most powerful production version of the Capri until the advent of the 1973-74 RS3100, the latter a machine we deal with in the following chapter, along with Ford's first fuel-injected road car, the RS2600. Engineering the 'Essex'-coded V6 into the Capri involved a large number of detail changes, including better bottom-end bearings, a more efficient sump oil pick-up and a

The ex-Ford Zodiac 'Essex' 3-litre V6 was considerably uprated in bottom-end strength and lubrication before its installation in the Capri, but a combination of wide gearbox ratios and a lazy induction provided performance that was initially little better than that of 2-litre V4 models. In October 1971, power was increased by at least 10bhp DIN and was transmitted through a gearbox with a longer second gear providing over 60mph.

system of baffles designed to cope with cornering forces measured at close to 1G on the standard 185/70 HR Grand Prix Goodyears that distinguished the same 5in rim steel wheels.

Available at prices from £1,341 upwards, the 3000GT generally came with all the XLR appendages and a bill for £1,427 12s 8d (£1,427.63). It was a justifiable premium over the lesser four-cylinder models for the V6 specification included a much stronger Zodiac Mark 4 manual gearbox with a Transit casing to adapt it for a floor gearchange instead of the Zodiac's column layout. Extra strength was evident within the body, particularly to cope with the additional engine weight at the front, where new chassis side rails were demanded and the top mounting points for the MacPherson struts were reinforced. The weight of the 3000GT was up by 263lb compared to the V4 at 2,380lb.

By 1971 the 3000GT was not only improved mechanically, but could also be obtained with better auxiliary lights, restyled sports steel wheels, the then fashionable fabric roof finish and a sunroof of the sliding steel type.

In October 1971 the increase in power of the 'Essex' V6 engine to 138bhp DIN increased the claimed top speed of the Capri 3000E, seen here, and the similarly powered 3000GT model, from 114mph to 122mph with a manual gearbox, or from 110mph to 118mph for cars equipped with automatic transmission.

First of the limited edition marketing-orientated specials were the orange 2000GT Capris with the Mustang via Lamborghini-inspired rear window slats and droopy tail spoiler. These were optional, but the colour, black vinyl roof and XLR pack were all part of the package to brighten up the 2000's languid image.

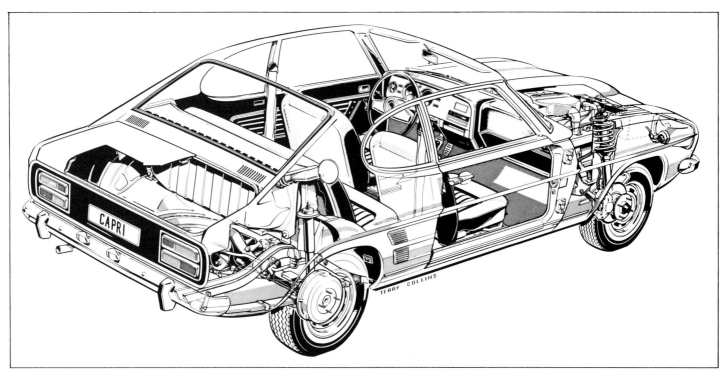

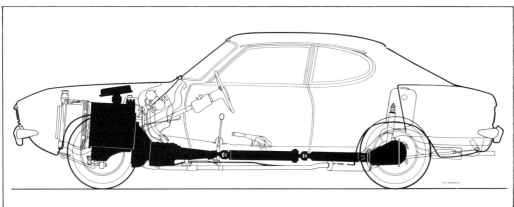

Terry Collins explains all in his usual exemplary cutaway drawing, above, this one in particular showing the autumn 1972 rear suspension change in which locating links were deleted in favour of an anti-roll bar. Also visible are the double strip tail lamps, new facia and revised steering wheel design adopted at the same time. Schematic side elevation from German press information, left, shows the disposition of the major mechanical elements in all Capris. The engine sat well back in the engine bay, passing power through the two-piece prop shaft to the leaf-sprung live axle.

This is Terry Collins' update of the original Capri drawing to show the Federal model's external modifications such as quadruple headlamps. Underneath, much the same mechanical parts could be used, including the top axle links. American-market Capris soon grew up from the in-line 1600 originals, like this one, to specially modified V6 motors before the 1977 decision to abandon US-market Capris, from which Cologne's production figures have never recovered.

The suspension was developed as well and set up with firmer rates than had been used previously: 122lb/in front and 125lb/in for the multiple-leaf rear suspension. For comparison, the 3-litre S and Ghia models of 1978 utilized MacPherson-strut spring rates of 106lb/in, mated to 123lb/in at the back of Ghias and 134lb/in for the S. (The latest Capri 2.8 Injection has the old 3-litre rate of 122lb/in up front and no less than 140lb/in from the single-leaf spring layout used at the rear, but one should remember that in recent years the increased use of gas-filled dampers has done more to alleviate the Capri's jarring ride than would have been possible in 1969.) The spring rate changes were accompanied by less pliable rubber mountings for the standard front anti-roll bar and firmer damper settings from Armstrong

and Girling, but the Mustang-style layout of staggering the rear shock absorbers — one in front and one behind the axle — remained a feature on this high-performance Capri.

Under the bonnet Ford put a larger radiator and battery, plus an air cleaner unique to this installation beneath the apparently necessary bonnet bulge. The latter spread further down range in later Capri life, but the twin-pipe exhaust of the V6 was always an identification aid.

Although fuel tank capacity was increased by 2 gallons to a total of 13.5 Imp gallons/62 litres, the braking performance was not seriously augmented. A half-inch on the rear linings and some anti-fade friction materials sufficed in the view of the company, so the solid 9.6in diameter front discs of this 114mph Capri were the same as for the basic 1600! Servo assistance was a standard feature of all Capris.

The engine was originally ascribed with 144bhp SAE at 4,750rpm, but subsequent investigation suggested that the true output was closer to 128bhp DIN, although this did not emerge until the V6 motor was uprated in October 1971. In *Autocar's* hands the original 3000GT was certainly a worthy pioneer of the Capri's enviable performance per £ spent reputation. It surged its way from standstill to 60mph in 10.3s, the rear tyres wreathed in blue smoke from its abrupt departure. Top speed was measured at 114mph and fuel consumption at 19.3mpg overall. *Motor* felt the car capable of only fractionally less than 111mph, with a 0-50mph capability of exactly 7 seconds, and they recorded 19.7mpg. As for the poor old MGB, it would take the Rover 3½-litre V8 to cheer that back to parity with the sporting Ford — and it took Leyland a few years to follow that logic, by which time the V6 Capris were firmly established, a contributory reason why the attractive MG V8 cocktail did not find the predicted commercial success.

Running changes

The 3000GT was not left at the top of the British range for long before Ford's E for Executive marketing suffix was applied to the Capri to produce a £1,541 3000E flagship. This carried all the usual XLR options, plus the then fashionable vinyl roof, the first cloth seat inserts to be offered in British Capris and the previously optional radio included in the increased price. These pushbutton devices were neatly incorporated as part of the facia, but they gave laughable reproduction and signal reception was often poor. Complete with opening rear windows (which boosted the throughput of the already efficient Aeroflow system quite remarkably) the 3000E was in production by November 1969 and on sale in March 1970.

By April, 250,000 Capris had been sold and on the third day of that month the Capri made its debut at the 1970 New York Show. At first only anaemic 1.6-litre models were sold in the USA, but then the Pinto overhead-camshaft motor made the trip back across the Atlantic in the Capri (the Pinto came from the American compact of that name, which had introduced a similar single-overhead-camshaft engine to the public in the 1960s). Eventually the Americans would have V6 Capris and would buy the model in huge numbers between 1970 and 1973 to maintain production over the 200,000 mark in each of those years. America took Capris only from the German plant after initial demand was served by Anglo-German sources and over half a million such Federal Capris had been delivered by August 1977, when export of the Mustang-inspired coupe ceased.

In Britain, September 1970 brought a useful, albeit small, power increase for the in-line four-cylinder power units of the 1300 and 1600 models. Power was now quoted in the more realistic DIN figures, and more of it had been extracted by inserting a slight combustion chamber in the cylinder heads, providing another new set of camshaft profiles and appropriately recalibrating the existing carburation. The basic 1300 gained 5bhp to start the range at 57bhp and the 1300GT was rated now at 72bhp, some 4bhp more than the ordinary 1600. The 1600GT now offered 86bhp, which was enough to provide 102mph and 0-60mph in 12s or less, according to Ford. At the time the 1600GT powerplant was one of the most widely used of all Ford engines, serving, for example, in the Escort Mexico, as well as providing the power base for Formula Ford racing. With the benefit of hindsight we can see why the Capri was allocated the 1600 crossflow so freely, for August 1970 was the date on which Ford launched the overhead-camshaft Cortinas, which had previously been the major users of the crossflow 1.6-litre engine. September 1970 also marked the introduction of better Lucas auxiliary lights, but the headlamps remained a weak point of the Capri until quadruple lamps were provided in a major facelift, two years later.

While 1970 was destined to stand as the all-time high for Capri production, confirming that both the American and the German markets were at their strongest for the novelty of the first 'European Mustangs', 1971 would see nearly 210,000 Capris made and a number of important changes made for the enthusiast. In October that year an extra 9lb/ft of torque and 10bhp were generated from the previously lazy V6 by a higher-lift and longer-duration camshaft operating enlarged inlet valves, plus totally reshaped inlet ports and larger jets in the twin-choke carburettor. Peak power, now 138bhp, moved from 4,750rpm to 5,000rpm, a tubular top manifold was fitted to the V6's cylinder banks, and the provision of a viscous-coupled fan completed the changes that made this model a 120mph vehicle, capable of reaching 60mph from rest in 8.2s according to my own fifth-wheel-measured figures of the time.

The running gear of this 3-litre model was further improved with the substitution of the 3.09:1 axle ratio for the original 3.22:1 and a longer second gear of 1.95:1. Now the Capri was geared at 21.8mph per 1,000rpm, which meant that the attainable 5,800rpm could provide 126.8mph under favourable circumstances. More importantly, the free-revving V6 would provide over 60mph in second gear to the considerable benefit of road performance. Other detail changes included a slightly softer rear suspension, an 8in diameter brake servo and new hubs that moved the 9.6in diameter discs outwards; the net result was a better feel to the brakes, although they were never a match for the 3-litre's pace.

October 1971 was also important for the deletion of the 1300GT from the range and the introduction of the flamboyant Vista Orange Capri Special. The first of many limited edition models, this was simply a 2000GT with a lot of E and XLR equipment incorporated, plus the rear window slats and bootlid-mounted 'wing' that were so widely copied by the British accessory industry — Ford having 'picked up' the slats from Lamborghini's Miura and inserted them on the Mustang a couple of years earlier!

In June 1972 the ordinary 1600GT's absence from the new car price lists since February of that year was explained when it joined the 2000 and 3000 models in another limited edition, and this time the less powerful models picked up the bonnet bulge that had served to identify the 3-litre for so long. Special colours — black with a red coachline was one very popular offering — distinguished these specials, which also spread the comfort of cloth trim a little further.

Major facelift

As production dropped below the 200,000 mark in 1972 it was no surprise that Ford should instigate a thorough overhaul of the model range in Britain and Germany for the autumn of that year. Some of the 150-odd changes Ford claimed would be carried over into the Capri II (the only Capri to be badged with a Mark number, although the terms Mark 1 and Mark 3 are commonly used to identify the first and third generation cars) notably the

A major redesign of the Capri's interior took place in September 1972, incorporating revised contouring for the front and rear seats for improved lateral and lumbar support, along with the provision of larger instruments within a new facia layout. This is the 3000GXL, with what was called a non-glare pebble-grain finish to the instrument panel.

Similar interior improvements were made to the Capri GT at the same time, but in this instance a matt black padded sports facia was provided. The former three-spoke steering wheel's replacement with an off-centre two-spoke design was a considerable aid to instrument visibility.

considerably softened suspension with an anti-roll bar running around the rear axle and picking up on the brackets used for the deleted rear radius arm mountings. On the 3-litre models the spring rates had dropped to 94lb/in front and 89lb/in rear, but a stiffer sports package was optional.

Another item — destined to carry over to the 1980s — was the revised dashboard, with larger and simplified instruments behind a two-spoke steering wheel the most obvious changes. Switchgear was changed, too, with a system that has partially survived to the present (particularly the central switches for the rear wiper and back screen demister), although the later proliferation of three steering column-mounted levers was preceded by this facelifted Mark 1's two-stalk system. New seating distinguished an interior that had the benefit and extra weight of further sound deadening. The viscous-coupled fan, with a maximum rpm of 2,700, was adopted for manual 3-litre models instead of just for the automatic-transmission versions. Ford then quoted 140bhp for what had become the 3000GXL, the new flagship being distinguished by the use of quadruple headlamps like those used by RS Capri derivatives, while in October 1972 all Capris had larger front and rear lamps and 5in-rimmed steel wheels. The new 3000GXL also received an important new gearbox, the Ford of Germany E-box which had grown up through the larger 2.6-litre models to become a standard fitment of the Granada range in April 1972. Complete with conventional top entrance for the gear-changing mechanism (the previous Zodiac-based four-speed box had demanded a more complex side-changing mechanism), Ford were able to fit a single-rail shifting mechanism that alleviated 90 per cent of the previous baulking and clanking that went on beneath a hard-driven 3-litre.

While the German models went over to overhead-camshaft engineering on all in-line four-cylinder models and had dispensed with their V4s entirely, Britain's Capri engine line for the facelifted model included just two 1600 overhead-camshaft units of Pinto descent. Thus the UK range began with the overhead-valve four-cylinder 'Kent' crossflow and then escalated into the 72bhp 1600 OHC and the twin-carburettor GT version of that engine, producing 88bhp from its 1,593cc. The V4 was retained despite the availability of the 2-litre OHC from the Cortina and the 3-litre 'Essex' V6 continued to head the British range.

The GXL version of the 3-litre Capri appeared in autumn 1972 and was the first volume-production Capri for the British and German markets to have quadruple headlamps, echoing the style first seen on the limited-production high-performance RS2600 in 1970.

September 1972 also marked the introduction of larger light units for the single-headlamp models, while the power bulge in the bonnet was no longer confined to 3-litre Capris.

Another identification feature of Capris introduced for the 1973 model year is the shorter mock air intake grilles ahead of the rear wheels. By way of contrast, the extractor vents for the ventilation system, beneath the rear screen, were strictly functional.

In October 1973 the UK market received the single-overhead-camshaft 1,593cc engine for the Capri, a unit which had previously been seen in the Cortina Mark 3.

At a guess the driver is Michael Bowler, then at *Motor,* but the picture's relevance is that by 1973 Broadspeed were able to offer customers a very exciting turbocharged version of the 3000 GXL. Ford Advanced Vehicles also had such a project under development, but the 210bhp result was confined primarily to producing 133mph and some 20mpg in an otherwise largely unmodified Cortina!

What might have been . . . . Unlike the Mustang, the Capri never appeared in a production convertible version, but this 1600XL was built for evaluation before the idea was abandoned.

As for prices, even the 1300 had scaled the £1,000 barrier handsomely in the three years and eight months that the car had been on sale and some 742,159 Capris had been sold in the first three years and five months. In September 1972 the Capri 1300 cost £1,206 with the rest of the range aligned as follows (note the deletion of the option packs, extra equipment now being incorporated where designated in the model title, although a sport pack could still be specified on some models): Capri 1600L, £1,285; 1600XL, £1,285; 1600GT, £1,464; 2000GT, £1,504; 3000GT, £1,763; 3000GXL, £1,966. Automatic transmission, which had been introduced as a near-£90 option in June 1970 for the 3000GT and 3000E, continued to be the Borg-Warner 35 three-speed unit, which would push the GXL over the £2,000 mark in 1972. Automatic transmission was also available for the V4 from Borg-Warner with Ford's own automatic, a rather better unit, coming into production for later 1600s.

In September 1972 Ford claimed a 0.40 drag factor for the revised Capris — all of which now shared the bonnet bulge and revised front-end styling — and the continuance of 1G cornering ability, despite the general softening in suspension and far wider use of rubber bushes to reduce noise levels and road-excited harshness. In summary, we can say that these were the softest-suspended and bushed Capris of the first series, the best equipped in terms of comfort and lighting, and with spectacular performance still available from the 3-litre.

In 1973, the full effect of this timely facelift could be seen when the British and German factories (the latter achieving the higher output from the start) got within 5,589 of the 1970 all-time record. On August 29, 1973 Capri production reached the million mark, and it fell to Ford's comparatively young Saarlouis works (situated close to the Franco-German border, where it had begun stamping out Escort and Capri panels in 1968) to produce the millionth car (a fuel-injected RS2600) some four-and-a-half years after the Capri was introduced. In December 1973, production of the two-door Capri came to an end, but that was not the end of the 'Mark 1' story. . . .

CHAPTER 3

RS2600 and RS3100

With competitions in mind, 1970 to 1974

The motivation behind the 1970-74 Ford Capri RS2600 — the company's first fuel-injected production car — and the carburated RS3100 model of 1973-74 was a simple need for a vehicle on which to base competition saloon cars. Such considerations governed basic items liked the engine capacity and the provision of a tail spoiler on the later car, because without 2,637cc the RS2600 could not have been enlarged to race at nearly 3 litres (at that time the rules only allowed cylinder bore increases) while the RS3100 could not race with the benefit of additional stability/traction offered by a rear spoiler had the RS3100 road car not had such an item in its standard equipment. Officially both models had to be produced in quantities of 1,000 per annum in order to qualify their competition cousins for International Group 2 saloon car racing events within the prestigious European Touring Car Championship. The Ford Motor Company are unlikely to reveal the precise production of RS2600 and RS3100 models (a policy they also follow regarding sporting Escorts), but personal experience at Ford Advanced Vehicle Operations, South Ockendon, Essex, the unit which was actually responsible for RS3100 output at Halewood, Liverpool, leads me to believe that Ford ordered up a lot more parts — such as Bilstein gas dampers and alloy wheels — than were ever needed in production. However, this was not because they were trying to deceive the sporting authorities, but because the pilfering rates were so high! A total of 248 original Capri RS3100s were delivered in 1973/74, according to Ford of Britain's internal statistics, a very small number indeed for a mass-production manufacturer.

So far as the RS2600 was concerned production was far more prolific, amounting to nearly 3,500 cars in four years and leading some optimists to say that the company should have applied for Group 1 competition recognition, which then required production of 5,000 cars a year! However, the specification of a Capri bearing an RS2600 badge varies considerably according to the period in which it was made, the first examples lacking the mechanical fuel-injection, proper wind-up window operation and glass, or even bumpers in the search for the all-important lightest racing weight possible.

In response to Ford Competition Manager Jochen Neerpasch's call for a 900kg (1,985lb) Capri of 2.6 litres to act as the roadgoing foundation for the Cologne-based Capri European racing programme, the first 50 RS2600s were completed by April 1970. Basically these amounted to German 2600GT Capris equipped with longer-throw crankshafts (90mm × 69mm instead of the GT's 90mm × 66.8mm) and ultra-light bodies. These lacked any heater or carpets and even the rear screen demister was omitted in the sacrifice to minimum weight. Perspex sliding panes substituted for roll-up door glass, the bumpers were deleted front and rear, and glass-fibre BBS panels were used for the bonnet, doors and bootlid. The bonnet was secured by pins and special thin glass was manufactured where Perspex could not be used. Even the paint process was special, for they knew that the various undercoats and primers, especially on the underbody, could account for over 30lb, so these Capris were sprayed with the bare minimum required to get a colour to adhere to their skimpy shell. All the early Capris I have seen pictured from this batch also used the magnesium Minilite road wheels for the same weighty reasons.

Neerpasch was given his desired ultra-lightweight road car and

Formidable on road or track, the Capri RS2600 was conceived very much with competition requirements in mind. After an initial batch had been made with carburettors, it became Ford's first fuel-injected European product. Nearly 3,500 RS2600s with injection were produced.

Later models used these FAVO-designed four-spoke aluminium wheels; usually the RS2600s were supplied on Pirelli CN 36-185 radial tyres.

Ford managed to hang on to this unrealistic racing weight for years. The proper production RS2600s, with their adaptation of Kugelfischer injection engineered by Weslake of Rye, in Sussex, weighed over 1,060kg (2,332lb), which was actually some 20kg (44lb) heavier than the normal German 2300/2600GT series!

Geneva debut

Engineering for the RS2600, as for other Rallye Sport products of that era, came from Britain, but production was always maintained in the Cologne pilot plant until true series production began and the model could be made at Saarlouis. Bob Howe was the head of a British department that included Rod Mansfield, Richard Martin-Hurst, Allan Wilkinson, Harry Worrall, Mike Cadby, Reg Chapman and Graham Parker. Mansfield supervised the field work, Worrall was the project engineer, Wilkinson acted as liaison engineer at the Cologne plant. Chapman and, later, apprentice Parker sorted out much of the fuel system detail that could not be covered by Weslake in the field.

Working from the new FAVO offices in South Ockendon, the small British team received the production approval for the

RS2600 in November 1969. By the following month the first rough prototypes had been constructed, but making a car that could be shown at the Geneva Show the following March for the official debut was a much harder task. It made the March 2, 1970 deadline, but only with a metallic mock-up of the unready fuel injection and through the initiative of Martin-Hurst (responsible for Anglo-German liaison on the project) who chartered a plane to fly the car across a snowy France.

As related, a small batch of Capris were made to enable the car to be recognized for competition in RS2600 guise from October 1970. Meanwhile, the production model, with its twin Cibié headlamp installation within the Federal twin-lamp accommodation, was approved on July 17, 1970 and approval for the mechanical parts was given the following month. September 14, 1970 saw the first of the injected production Capris leave the line . . . but it didn't go very far! Because of the wider wheels and revised engine bay crossmember (which provided extra front wheel negative camber), the tyres were found to foul the bodywork on lock. Extra clearance was needed, leading to the distinctive flare of the production RS2600 wheelarch at the front,

An 'Injection' logo was carried on the bonnet and at the rear [which had no spoiler, much to the detriment of racing versions], while the fuel filler flap of this 1972 model carried a legend incorporating '2600', 'Injection' and 'RS' in a roundel. The most popular colour scheme was a white body with blue contrasting panels; bumpers were matt black years before the practice spread to mainstream vehicles such as Escort Populars!

a modification arranged and implemented via the Niehl, Cologne, pilot plant in one week instead of the months that such a late modification would normally require.

Original specification

Weslake drew and had made cast aluminium components to form the plenum chamber above the new inlet tracts for the injection, the pump for which was mounted outboard of the left-hand cylinder bank (looking from the front) and connected to the front crankshaft pulley by a small cogged-belt drive. Originally there was no cold-start mixture provision and the injection cam was sensitive only to throttle opening and engine rpm, but when the car was in full production both a cold-start injection mechanism and a camshaft for the injection that also took account of manifold vacuum pressure were provided.

For the road cars Weslake did not have to supply the aluminium cylinder heads that were to form a basic part of the racing specification, so a siamese-pipe top exhaust manifold could be retained. This fed into single pipes that ran on either side beneath the Capri, feeding through two separate silencer boxes per side before emerging separately with a distinctive oval exhaust tailpipe redolent of some performance Mustangs.

Aside from the longer-stroke iron crankshaft, the 2.6-litre V6 received 10:1 compression pistons of shorter overall depth and the higher-performance 2300GT Capri camshaft, which had been

an essential part of extracting 125bhp instead of 108bhp from 2.3 litres. The sump was a modified 2300 pan, while the flywheel came from the large Taunus 26M saloon. In its original lightweight form triple Solex carburettors were employed and there was mention of 160bhp for the road. However, like the 2.8 injection of 10 years later, the RS2600 became an official 150bhp Capri in later production, maximum power being developed at up to 5,800rpm. Peak torque, some 159lb/ft, was reported at 4,000rpm. In practice this meant that the RS2600 had a good 20bhp more than the yet to be developed British 3-litre, but not so much lazy torque. In a straight line the lightweight versions could cover a standing quarter-mile in under 16s, but the more usual figures were for 0-62mph (100km/h) in 8.6s and a maximum speed of 124mph, almost 10mph faster than the British 3-litre of the period.

Finished in the works racing silver-and-blue colours of 1970, the first Capri RS2600s came to market with the Taunus 26M gearbox and a modified clutch from the same source. The final-drive ratio was 3.22:1, as used for pre-October 1971 Capri 3-litres. The Ford rear axle and drive-shafts proved exceptionally strong over the years and were one of the few components to escape replacement, even in such violent racing models as the earlier Zakspeed Turbo Capris and the 440bhp Capri-Cosworth machines.

As introduced the brakes were simply those of lesser V6 Capris,

Ford Advanced Vehicles, Weslake and Kugelfischer were all involved in the development and manufacture of the RS2600 fuel-injected V6.

The injection 2.6-litre engine photographed in a 1971 model. The layout of the 150bhp unit was neatly executed, including the provision of special exhaust top manifolds in tubular steel.

but the suspension was certainly special. At the front there was a short and stiff coil spring around the uprated MacPherson strut with a thicker anti-roll bar. The lower front suspension arm picked up at a point slightly outboard of that provided on a normal production crossmember, while the back axle was suspended by a single-leaf spring on either side. The loss of the multiple leaves saved a little more weight and the single leaf seemed to locate the axle better against sideways forces; this feature has stood the test of time with many RS-branded products using the single-leaf rear-end, as also did the 2.8i. Low and stiff summarized the suspension approach, but the result was not quite so uncomfortable as might have been expected, thanks to Bilstein gas-filled damping front and rear.

Apart from the small batch made with Minilites, the first RS Capris for the road wore Richard Grant cast-aluminium 6J × 13 road wheels with a grey finish to distinguish them from the shiny silver wheels Grant offered to the public. Specified tyres were Goodyear Rallye Special 185/70 HR—13s, but I also tested cars

Hella halogen headlamps adorn the bumperless front of this original lightweight Capri RS2600.

Better seating

The interior was very thoroughly improved by the standards of the 1970s, using more supportive front seats and matching their comfortable cord trim facings with new inserts for the back seat trim as well. Today, a sporting finish is taken for granted, along with sports seating, in models like the Escort XR3i, but in the Britain of the 1970s you were lucky to get more than a pint of matt black paint and a GT badge with a sporting saloon. So the idea of a sports model that offered extra comfort as well as extra speed, handling and braking was then fresh enough for legends to grow up around the Ford newcomer in much the same way as had happened with the Mini-Cooper S and Lotus Cortina.

Adding to an interior already blessed with Scheel reclining front seats was a deeply dished Springall FordSport steering wheel of the kind used on works Escorts for so many years. It had a soft leather rim and sat in front of a standard 2600GT facia, which included a 220km/h speedometer and a 7,000rpm tachometer that was redlined just below 6,000rpm (the 2600GT barely preceding the RS2600 on the German market, for it was announced in August 1970 with 125bhp). Complementing the leather-rim steering wheel was the use of the same material for the gearlever knob, a luxury they felt they could afford, even on the first lightweights. However, a gearlever console, normally part of a V6 Capri in Britain or Germany, was out of the question until the inevitable later model-year improvements began to creep the weight and specification back towards a softer road car approach. Incidentally, on the original batch of lightweight cars the sporting recliner seats were deleted in favour of full-blooded, fixed-back, competition seats.

By October 1971 we could see that the late Mike Cadby had been working on a much more civilized and better-braked RS2600. Important mechanical changes included a Granada gearbox with its closer second-to-third gear ratios and the installation of the 3.09:1 final drive, allowing just over 20mph per 1,000rpm in top gear. FAVO cast-alloy wheels with four spokes provided more accommodation behind their further offset centres to house ventilated front disc brakes of 9.75in diameter. These were made up from some specially supplied discs, originally intended for a 3-litre V6 Cortina which never made FAVO production, and the Granada callipers. The hubs had to be specially fabricated, making it a very expensive Capri brake

from the 1970-71 era on Pirelli CN 36s to the same dimensions.

The 9.6in diameter solid discs and larger rear drums of the 2600GT/Capri 3-litre were employed on the 1970 RS2600, anti-fade linings and pads from Ferodo being included as part of a specification that initially included a 7in diameter servo-assistance unit. Later RS Capris used the 8in brake booster in a useful further example of Anglo-German co-operation, for the bigger unit came from Britain.

The interior of these two 1970 and 1971 Capri RS2600s emphasizes that sporting seating and a new steering wheel can do much to enhance the appearance of a cockpit. Later models had a flat steering wheel and revised, although still superior seating. Note the use of leather for the gear-lever knob.

conversion if attempted by private owners of 3-litre cars, which remained on the solid discs until their demise in 1981.

Externally, the RS2600 grew the familiar Ford performance identity of front quarter-bumpers (a Lotus Cortina/Escort Twin-Cam and RS1600 characteristic) and a rear bumper. The front quarter-bumpers allowed installation of the flashing indicators, which had previously been set into the lower valances. The useful quadruple Cibié quartz-iodine headlamps remained, to disgrace the appalling standards of lesser production models, and the external look of the RS2600 from October 1971 began to reflect increasing use of body stripes and RS identification. By 1974 the rear-end had its own stripe carrying the words 'Injection' on one side and 'RS' added on the other. From the front the traditional Capri use of a contrasting colour for the bonnet was set off with a stripe around the bonnet bulge carrying the 'Injection' motif on one side and the lettering 'RS2600' on the driver's side. By the end of the model run (ie for the 1973-74 model-year) the RS2600 had predicted another later sporting cliché — the use of a matt black finish for the bumpers.

In October 1971 softer settings were introduced for the Bilstein dampers along with normal road coil springs for the front MacPherson struts. Prior to this the RS had used whatever could be found in the competition parts bin on the suspension side, but now the ride height had risen it was hard to see any difference between GT and RS models, although we were assured that the RS2600 always rode at least an inch lower.

The RS2600 continued its production life with the 2.6-litre injected engine giving good service once the automatic choke had been incorporated (it was on the standard equipment list by August 1970). There was an initial problem with the timing of the six-element injection pump for early production models, but once this had been sorted out both it and the high-pressure electric gear pump usually performed reliably.

The RS2600 was sold with left-hand drive only. After initial sales had been confined to Germany, or to the supply of lightweights to competition personnel overseas (Francois Migault in Monaco, John Fitzpatrick and, later, Gerry Birrell in Britain), sales in Europe began properly in 1971 and the model proved popular amongst enthusiasts in France and Belgium. There were occasional mutterings of FAVO in Britain bringing the RS2600 to market in right-hand drive form, but former South Ockendon

executive Kevin Cooney was able to tell me why Britain never had such a Capri. 'Basically it was a question of the strength of the 3-litre Capri in Britain. The sales were still strong and profitability was better in a 3-litre unit than for the RS2600.' So Britain never joined France, Belgium, Italy (where special headlamps were required) and Switzerland on the export list, but both Vice-President, Public Affairs, Walter Hayes and Ford Advanced Vehicle Operations Director, Stuart Turner operated converted RHD RS2600s during 1973-74.

Just as motor racing needs had dictated the presence of an RS2600 in the Ford price list, so the same sport was to demand an end to its life and its replacement with an engine over 3 litres, plus a rear spoiler. This time, both the engineering and the production would come from Britain.

RS3100 rationale

The 1972 European Touring Car Championship racing season was dominated by Capri RS2600s equipped with Weslake-modified 3-litre versions of the German V6 motor. Even at the height of their success steps were being taken by Ford's sporting management that would shape an almost frightening leap forward in the coupe's competition potential. On May 1, 1972 Jochen Neerpasch and Martin Braungart, the key figures in the administration and technical progress of the racing Capris, joined BMW Motorsport, in Munich! Later that month, Cosworth senior designer Michael Hall began drawing up a large-capacity, four-valve-per-cylinder, DOHC version of the British Ford 3-litre 'Essex' V6 engine. It was a power unit that would be asked to provide well over 400bhp by 1974, when the Group 2 Touring Car regulations would admit racing cylinder heads for production engines, providing the car makers ensured the production of at least 100 such head kits.

Michael Kranefuss was chosen to succeed Jochen Neerpasch as Ford Competition Manager and he, prompted by the worries of his star Capri drivers regarding tail-end lift at the 160mph-plus maximum of the 1971 Capris at Le Mans, began to push for a production Capri with a tail spoiler. However, it was a subject that Ford of Germany and their partners in British sporting management just did not seem to be able to progress. The British appeared to the Germans to be totally preoccupied with their Escort rallying successes, yet the newly appointed British

During 1973 the over-bored RS3100 Capri took shape. Halogen quad lamps, front spoiler [already kerbed on this example!] and pronounced negative camber for the Goodyear-shod front wheels were shared with the RS2600 of the period.

Competition Manager (succeeding Stuart Turner, who went down to South Ockendon in 1972 to manage FAVO that summer) was Peter Ashcroft. Peter knew the Capri's problems from the inside as he had been seconded to Ford of Germany to find a practical answer to the racing team's engine unreliability problems prior to the 1971 season.

Looking back with the benefit of a decade's hindsight, it appears to me that Ford decided to buy their way out of the Capri's increasing technical inferiority versus the revitalized 1973 BMW team with copious helpings of driver talent (including Jackie Stewart and others who are recalled in Chapter 5) rather than modify the production RS2600 with a tail spoiler. Whatever, it was September 1973 before the product planning department at FAVO could provide a production authorization for the Capri

that would carry the key elements in Ford's bid to wrest back European supremacy from BMW in 1974 (the Munich company under Neerpasch had won all but two races in the 1973 European Championship).

The model was the RS3100 and it amounted to a 1973 RS2600 chassis and brakes accommodating a 95.19mm × 72.42mm over-bored version of the 3-litre V6 plus a large ducktail air dam on the bootlid. This use of a maximum service bore (the production 3.0 V6 had a 93.7mm bore) allied to the standard stroke provided 3,091cc instead of 2,994cc. Research at Cosworth and other outside engine specialists, plus Ford's own knowledge of the meaty 'Essex' V6, had indicated that their 3-litre production engine could be run at anything up to 3.7 litres, but all that was necessary for the most efficient racing power/ reliability equation

For the carburated British successor to the RS2600, little luxuries like individual exits for the exhausts on either side of the car were dispensed with on the RS3100. Striping was as for the RS2600, but with the injection lettering deleted. The basic body and trim came mostly from the Capri 3000GT.

All bulges, bumps and spoilers! A prototype RS3100 seen with the vital competition 'ducktail' prominently displayed.

Credited with just under 150bhp, the RS3100 was independently tested to maximum speeds beyond 120mph, yet was usually found able to produce fuel consumption figures at least on a par with its standard 3-litre counterpart, indicating a significant improvement in efficiency.

was 3.4 litres, obtainable via a vast 100mm bore and the mandatory production 72.42mm stroke.

Externally the RS3100 engine wore blue rocker covers to signify the extra performance, but beneath them there was little extra work aside from the marginal capacity stretch. The standard Weber twin-choke carburettor fed the engine through cylinder head ports that were meant to flow slightly more mixture to the maximum service size pistons, which boosted compression slightly over the production 9:1.

Ford staff from Boreham ran six prototype cars around the RAC Rally route that November with a variety of further engine modifications, including pre-production RS3100s with up to 165bhp available from more vigorous camshaft timing and complete dual-pipe exhaust systems, the latter providing an extra 5-8bhp in themselves. However, this was an expensive enough project for the company to make a limited number of special

Capris at a mass-production plant, and for the RS3100 they chose to do this at Halewood, Liverpool, so the engine modifications were destined not to include the camshaft and exhaust sophistications. Maximum power was quoted as 148bhp at 5,000rpm rather than the 140bhp at 5,300rpm for the V6 3-litre of the period with viscous-coupled fan, while torque for the RS3100 was reported as 187lb/ft at the same 3,000rpm peak as for the normal 3-litre's 174lb/ft maximum.

The four-speed transmission and 3.09:1 final-drive ratio of the 3-litre Capri remained unaltered, and the basic starting point for these right-hand-drive-only cars was the Capri 3000GT, but equipped with the quadruple headlamps of 3000GXL, which were not quite in the same bracket as the RS2600's Cibiés, but were a distinct improvement nevertheless.

The RS3100 road cars used some of the RS2600's later external striping, but naturally with the lettering removed. The bumpers

One of the original 3.1-litre RS3100 pre-production Capris shows off its distinctive white striping against the contemporarily popular blue paintwork. Note that it lacks the production quarter-bumpers, but has the proper spoilers. This car was one of the half-dozen that covered the 1973 RAC Rally route.

were as specified for the RS2600 in matt black, but some of the pre-production run counted for homologation purposes had chrome bumpers and even, in one case, rectangular headlamps!

Body colours for production RS3100s were those of the 1973 FAVO Escort RS range, which meant Diamond White, Daytona Yellow, Sebring Red, Olympic Blue, Modena Green, Marine Blue and — a real piece of Ford marketing descriptive prose — Stardust (metallic). Incidentally, the production side stripe that traces out the 'hockey stick' styling crease on each side of an RS3100 was derived from a sports decal pack that Ford offered at the time.

Black figured largely in the external paint scheme and was the finish adopted for the simple blade RS2600-type front spoiler (fitted in production for the German car in the 1972 model-year). Interior trim, black again, was as for the standard 3-litre and included a two-spoke steering wheel, although the press cars and many privately owned RS3100s were fitted with the more appropriate RS three-spoke design, its convoluted-can safety structure and 14in diameter having proved very satisfactory in crash tests.

However, RS2600 equipment that did make the trip across the Channel included the valuable ventilated 9.75in diameter front disc brakes and the negative camber crossmember for a similar Bilstein-damped suspension system; only 'similar' because the softer Directors Settings were selected for the gas dampers. Spring rates were a hard 142lb/in front and 112lb/in for the single-leaf rear-end, providing a ride height of 50.37in instead of the 50.9in quoted in the Ford 3-litre Capri homologation form for competitions at that time. The RS3100 also picked up the 2600's four-spoke 6J × 13 cast-alloy road wheels and the axle bump rubbers that prevented the ultimate discomfort when the short-travel rear suspension had bottomed out under a full passenger load and vigorous motoring.

Aerodynamic tests at the Motor Industry Research Association (MIRA) facility in Britain recorded the best ever drag coefficient on record for the original Capri series (0.375 Cd). It seems quite possible in the light of subsequent Ford figures for Capri Cd factors that this was the most slippery Capri production shape of all time, being significantly narrower than the 'Mark 3s', for which a 0.374 Cd was claimed in 1978 S-guise.

Tail-end of a pre-production RS3100 with the boot lock tucked into the striped tail and deformable plastic spoiler. This Capri ran with a non-production camshaft and larger bore tailpipes to generate around 160bhp with good flexibility.

Thus, although the RS3100 did not represent the technical step forward that the RS2600 had embodied in its pioneering use of fuel-injection on a European Ford — nor did it have so many of the sporting creature comforts with its largely standard interior — it was still a significantly improved Capri. The rear spoiler not only helped the racers, but provided a measure of motorway crosswind stability that Capris had always lacked, and the better brakes were long overdue in Britain.

As for performance, the UK road-testers spoke of up to 124mph and 0-60mph in around 8s. Most seemed pleased with the fuel consumption in relation to the performance and reports of up to 22mpg were common. Certainly 100mph cruising was possible, with far more stability than before, with the reassuring thought that the brakes stood a much better chance of stopping the Capri from these speeds than had been the case for the 3-litres.

The Ford Capri RS3100 was accepted into Group 2 for international motor sport on January 1, 1974, barely a month before Ford announced an entirely new three-door body for the Capri! Priced at £2,450, it would compete for sales against the BMW 2002 (£2,399), Alfa Romeo 2000 GTV (£2,849) and 3½-litre MGB GT V8 (£2,294). Yet it was all too late. In the wake of the fuel crisis of the time, motor sport events of the calibre of the Monte Carlo Rally were being cancelled and by December 1974 the British FAVO factory itself would be shut and Ford competitions activity in Germany officially curtailed. The Arab-Israeli war and subsequent oil embargoes had led Western Europe quickly into a recession and had provoked earnest thoughts about the price and finite availability of oil which have constituted a basic car design parameter ever since.

Yet for Ford in Europe and America the Capri tale was far from over. They might have announced a fire-breathing 120mph-plus sports coupe at exactly the wrong moment — a gaffe they shared with BMW — but that old Ford friend, market research, had thrown up a new twist to the Capri theme at precisely the right time.

CHAPTER 4

Capri II: 1974 to 1978

A third door and a new image

Complete with its jaunty red decals on the back panel proclaiming that this was indeed the 'II' version of 'The car you always promised yourself', the Capri II was born officially upon an unhappy British market in February 1974. 'Unhappy', because many potential customers were more preoccupied by queueing for fuel at their previously friendly local dealership rather than in the outlay of between £1,731 and £3,109 for the new three-door Capri II range. Production during the launch year was almost up to the levels of the previous model — nearly 184,000 Capri IIs were made in Britain and Germany during 1974 — but by 1975 output had slumped dramatically, the 100,050 Capris made in that year representing less than half of the totals for the original Capri in 1969, 1970, 1971 and 1973. Although initial reaction to the concept of a third door in the sporty coupe was good, production sagged rapidly during the Capri II run. By 1977 output was down by 92,119 units on the 1974 introduction figure and it was obvious that further changes would be needed if the German market in particular was to absorb any significant further Capri sales.

In assessing the model in terms of numbers sold, the motoring historian might well dub the Capri II the commercial failure amongst the recent coupes to bear this name, but the truth — as ever — is a little more complicated. In fact the Capri II's third door and attention to family needs concerning luggage space, better ride, improved visibility and lower noise levels were welcomed warmly in the UK. Sales in Britain in 1976 were over double those recorded for Capri II in Germany.

Yet neither Britain nor Germany and the rest of the European market could prevent Capri economics suffering the most enormous blow of all — the end of Capri production for the USA. This occurred in August 1977, after the USA had taken 513,449 original-body and Federalized Capri IIs since the New York Show introduction of the former model in April 1970.

Just as significant to British interests during the Capri II run was the decision to transfer all Capri manufacture to Germany in October 1976. Some 337,491 Capris had been made in the Halewood plant at Liverpool, but the transfer of Halewood production to Germany seemed inevitable once the volumes started slipping and economics dictated one-factory manufacture. Given that the British production rate lagged significantly behind that in Germany — a problem frequently publicized by Ford in connection with Escort output at the identically equipped Halewood and Saarlouis plants — it seemed inevitable that Ford would transfer all Capri production to Germany rather than the other way around. (British factory workers argued that Ford in Germany had been given all the plum jobs, like the Federal Capri run, which in 1971 had enabled them to make nearly 169,000 Capris compared with just 41,113 in Britain.) A turning point came when they started making the 3000GXL to head the German range as well as that of the UK (with the 1972 facelift of the original Capri that included the larger lamps). Gradually, more and more of the luxury or sporting models in the Ford range would be 'Made in Germany' to give extra cachet to the UK buyer of Ghia, S or the RS Escort models following the 1974 closure of FAVO at South Ockendon.

Specification details

There really was more of everything in the Capri II, but

Capri IIs that might have been. Design work started on Capri variants to give more passenger and luggage room not long after the public launch of the 1969 model. Here we see solutions that echo Ford's American Pinto hatchback, a very clean model that almost loses the fastback element in the Capri's style completely, and the flared-arch approach, complete with a hint of Alfa Romeo Montreal front-end style.

The suspension of the hatchback Capri II remained the same as on later versions of the original-shape model, as did the facia. Note however that the fuel tank had to move from behind the rear seats to the underfloor area aft of the axle, a source of considerable development difficulty.

features like the extra weight (up 200lb in comparable 1969 and 1974 3000GT guise) and fatter dimensions lessened the appeal to enthusiasts faced with a new generation of coupes from VW and GM during the life of Capri II.

Dimensionally the difference could be summarized as a larger car carrying three times more luggage, in Ford's estimation, on the same 100.8in wheelbase. Up went body width from 64.8in to 66.85in, along with a stretch from 50.2in to 51.14in in the quoted

height of the 3000GT. In overall length Ford quoted 168.83in without bumper overriders and 170.9in when these were included. Originally, the 3000GT was quoted as being 167.8in long in the owner's manual, but Ford press material quoted 169.4in. Either way, they resisted the temptation to insert an American-style stretch such as was a regular feature of Mustangs before the rush to small cars in the later-1970s.

There were significant plus points to the Capri's width and

weight growth. The third-door layout was one of the best seen in Europe, incorporating individual folding squabs on the rear seats for more expensive models (others had a one-piece folding bench seat), and a smooth action for the heavy back door, supported by two gas-filled struts. Around the rear door Ford built a strengthening cage structure, partly to support the hatch and partly to offset the loss in body stiffness engendered by cutting a large hole in the previously hunched metal hindquarters.

If you compare the lines of the 1969 Capri and the 1974 model it quickly becomes apparent that Ford's main bonus in glass area — a frequently quoted 14 per cent over the two-door coupes — came from the larger glass panel in the rear hatchback. However, there was also a bonus from the lower glass line offered within the front two doors and the rear side screens, but the windscreen area remained as before.

From a safety aspect, the Capri II displayed significant progress over its predecessor. Visibility was better thanks to the rear door and lowered side glass area, and some of the extra weight went into double-skinning the three-quarter rear panels and the provision of closed box sections to reinforce the areas around the doors and on the roof, to improve roll-over protection. By this stage, over 500 crash tests of varying intensity had been carried out by the company — and a lot more by the customers!

From a primary safety viewpoint, and to the great benefit of those who wanted extra rear-end stability from the Capri under full-power cornering conditions, the rear track was increased from 52in to 54.5in and the front was fractionally wider on the newer Capri at 53.3in versus 53in. When a later generation of Goodyear Grand Prix radials became available, together with gas-filled rear dampers, the excessive tail-threshing progress of a hard-driven original 3000GT became a memory. However, on a damp road a V6 Capri still needed respect and careful application of power if the driver wished to stay away from the temptations of hedging and ditching in the early stages of ownership.

A welcome improvement in braking resources was the fitment of 9.75in (247.5mm) diameter disc brakes at the front of 3-litre models in the UK, although the rest of the range, bar the plain 1300, utilized 9.625in (244mm) discs as before. The rear brakes on the V6 models remained at a healthy 9in diameter and 2.25in lining width, the same diameter but 1.7in width being utilized for the remainder of the range bar the 1300, which was the only

Capri II without servo-assistance as standard. The 1300 used a 9.5in (241mm) front disc and an 8in by 1.45in rear drum, as before.

Radial-ply tyres were standard throughout the new Capri range, resting on rims no smaller than 5J × 13in, even in the case of the 1300. A 165-13 tyre was the standard fitting for all but 3-litre models, but a widely adopted option was the 3-litre's 185 HR-13 rubber. Only the top Capri Ghia 3.0 offered a wider wheel width and aluminium construction as standard equipment — the familiar multi-spoke 5½J × 13 design that was destined to last into 1981.

Before we discuss the range and individual model equipment it is worth recalling that the Capri II represented a host of detail changes in design and engineering work that dated back to 1970. It is easy to overlook the importance of the September 1972 facelift of the original model, which introduced over 151 modifications that carried over into the new sheet metal, including the revised suspension and new facia, plus the larger lamps at the front, which gave us more than an inkling of how the Capri II would feel and look on the road. Ford reckoned that 2,000 new or developed parts had gone into Capri II, along with over 186,000 test miles at the company's giant Belgian test track in Lommel and more than 2 million man-hours.

Ghia luxury

There were eight basic models in the 1974 Capri II range, which had grown far closer to their German equivalents than was originally the case. The British line were badged as follows: 1300L, 1600L, 1600XL, 1600GT, 2000GT, Ghia 2.0, 3000GT and Ghia 3.0. The Ghia name meant much more than just a tacked on badge à la GT school of marketing. Ford had acquired an interest in the Italian coachbuilding concern at Turin in 1970 and converted this to full ownership in December 1972. By this stage the first production car credited to Ford and Ghia had already held a rather uncertain claim to enthusiasts' affections — the Pantera V8 of De Tomaso ancestry.

Ford's objective in acquiring Ghia was to try to inject a worthwhile luxury bonus into their production car line — one of sufficient showroom ostentation as to attract a considerable price premium over the rest of the range. Today we have Ghia models of every Ford in the range, but the Granada and the Capri were

The changes in top sheet metal were extensive, even the side doors being affected by the increase in glass area, although the windscreen remained as before. Built on the original wheelbase, the Capri II was 2.1in wider and nearly an inch longer and higher.

the earliest examples in Europe.

Ironically, Ghia's first mass-production brief was an upmarket version of Mustang II launched in September 1973. Time and again Ghia have managed to produce a new Ford concept from drawing board to metal at such a pace that the company has been able to see what an idea — such as a mid-engined Escort — feels like on the road only months after somebody in management wondered aloud about the feasibility of such a project.

For the Capri II the Ghia outfit worked with the designers at the Ford Cologne-Merkenich centre to provide a number of unique features. Frequently some of the more individual thinking was rejected, but the result was a Capri resting on unique alloy wheels with a far plusher interior than any European Ford had previously offered. Using a cloth upholstery known as Rialto, the

Despite fastback styling, the hatchback Capri II extended the Capri's carrying capacity and mass appeal considerably. The problem was that many saw the heavier newcomer as a family rather than a sporting car and its appeal waned rapidly, particularly in Germany.

Capri Ghia had a heavily padded look applied to the seating and door trim panels, although they did without the wood trims that would become part of the Ghia tradition from the Granada onwards. Other exclusive Ghia features included cut-pile carpets that crept up the lower door trim panels and a padded finish for the facia. A sliding steel sunroof, a vinyl roof and a better quality radio were also part of the original Capri Ghia deal, along with some metallic paint finishes that drew favourable comment, particularly the grey.

Mechanically the Capri Ghias were available only with the top two amongst the unchanged five Capri engines. In Britain this meant either the 138bhp 'Essex' 3-litre V6 or the SOHC in-line 2-litre four-cylinder producing 98bhp. In Germany the 3-litre V6 topped the range — the RS2600 unit unfortunately having been superseded by the change to Capri II and by the sporting need for the RS3100 which was still straggling out of Halewood and into the showrooms after the launch of Capri II. In both Germany and Britain the 3-litre unit was used with its attendant Granada

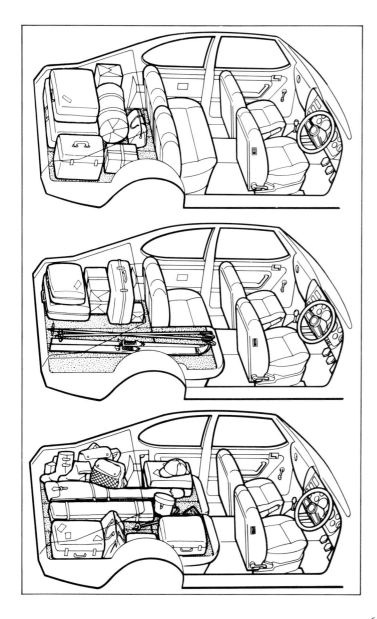

gearbox for Ghia and GT models, plus subsequent derivatives like the S. In Germany there had always been a preference for V6 power over the rather rough but mechanically more efficient SOHC 2-litre four, and in 1974 this manifested itself by the Germans omitting the smaller engine, of Pinto descent, in favour of their own 2.3-litre V6. This preference was still evident in the 1980s with a 90bhp 2-litre V6 being used instead of the 100bhp four, even though the latter unit had a demonstrable fuel consumption advantage.

The 1,993cc SOHC four was fresh to the British Capri range, but had been used from August 1970 in the Mark 3 Cortina; oddly enough, the Germans used the unit briefly from the Autumn 1972 facelift of the original Capri until the arrival of Capri II, when they went back to the beloved Cologne V6 family.

In the UK the 2-litre powered some Ghias and the 2000GT and has since proved one of the most popular Capri choices amongst enthusiasts, combining nearly 105mph with 26-28mpg, even in brisk use. Acceleration from 0-60mph in Capri II trim was quoted at 10.5s, which was certainly quick enough to qualify for a sporting performance at the time. The balance between speed, mpg and insurance rate was, and remains, more likely to suit the younger enthusiast driver with V6 aspirations but a four-cylinder cheque book.

There were three 1.6-litre models in Britain, all using the overhead-camshaft engine rather than the previous 'Kent' crossflow unit. The 1600GT utilized a twin-choke Weber carburettor and benefited from better manifolding and a more lively camshaft profile than its lesser 1600 sisters to provide 88bhp at 5,700rpm. In practice, this meant that the 1600GT was a little below par for a car with sporting aspirations and 1.6 litres, having to haul 2,326lb, which was only 22lb less than the far more torquey 2-litre; it would achieve 100mph only under favourable conditions and 0-60mph took the best part of 13s or more. Rowed along in spirited style, the 1600GT was unlikely to show a fuel consumption benefit over the 2-litre as the engine was being worked harder to maintain an equivalent pace. However, the driver who merely wanted the occasional extra sparkle of a 1600GT over the single-choke-carburated 1600L and XL models

Making the most of the hatchback and individual rear seat folding mechanism with the 1974 Capri II interior.

61

A 1600GT version of the Capri II was offered from the February 1974 launch date of the rebodied range with an 88bhp version of the four-cylinder engine. However, the GT badge was only to survive on Capris for a few months after the introduction of the S models the following year.

(offering 72bhp at 5,200rpm) could find it a welcome choice with the chance of over 30mpg when driven moderately.

A Capri 1300L started the British Capri II range at well under £2,000 and offered a rather anaemic 57bhp to propel 2,227lb. According to *Autocar* performance data this dynamic introduction to Capri II motoring offered an 86mph maximum, coupled to 0-60mph in 18.8s. Their overall mpg figure was 28.7, which reflects again how the smaller-engined Capris really have to work for a living. However, for the man who just wanted the three-door body and a shape that was different to next door's Cortina, there

was a ready UK market to satisfy, and the addition of the hatchback began what was to be a lifesaving number of sales to the business market.

The German engines rated slightly differing power outputs in some cases, despite the common use of all engines in the Capri II range except the 108bhp V6 of 2,294cc — later to be a very familiar unit to British Cortina and Granada buyers, uprated in the 1979 model-year to 114bhp and eventually to be installed in the 1982 Sierra. The 2.3 V6 has never been offered to UK Capri buyers, but it makes a very nice motorway cruiser with its smooth

A plush interior with colours carefully coordinated was an essential factor in the Ghia models from the beginning. Quite what use the passenger grab handle is above the glove box is beyond this writer . . . You can also learn a little of Ford Photographic's pioneering spirit from this picture since this is also the first and last Capri Ghia II·without a roof!

power delivery and 130lb/ft of torque, and it saves a little fuel over the 3-litre. Top speed is approximately 110mph in a Capri II body with 0-60mph in 10s.

In Britain three gearboxes were used to serve the Capri II range, with the Ford C3 automatic (manufactured at Bordeaux) available as an option on all models other than the 1300L. The 1300, 1600S and 1600GT all used the same gearbox, one shared with the German 1300. Then, for the British 2-litres and all German Capri IIs of 1.6 to 3.0 litres, there was the common ex-Cortina/Taunus gearbox with the usual Granada ratio set shared amongst the 3-litres. Ratios will be found in the appendices.

For the final-drive ratios the British and German engineers had both started with 4.125:1 (16.26mph per 1,000rpm) for the 1300 and graduated to the usual 3.09:1 (21.86mph per 1,000rpm) for

the 3-litre.

Vacuum-servo assistance for the steering rack-and-pinion layout was offered only when full production of the 3-litre models was reached, some months after the official introduction date. The steering ratio remained at 17.4:1, giving a 32ft turning circle via the 15in diameter two-spoke steering wheel of the 1972 facelift Capri.

Equipment and options
As ever, the suffixes spelt important differences in the level of standard equipment offered on various Ford models. For example, you did not get a radio until a Ghia was ordered; otherwise, Ford radios remained options in 1974 and the same remark applied to a laminated windscreen and to the excellent

Two more overhead views of the same cutaway car, showing the versatility of the passenger and luggage accommodation, something which was always an important plus point for the three-door Capri and made it a more practical proposition than the original version.

A picture which emphasizes the useful storage length obtainable when the rear seats of a Capri II are folded forwards. Inevitably, both height and width were restricted by the Capri's sporty character and intrusive rear dampers.

steel sliding roof.

Beginning with the 1300 and 1600L, the basic Capri II specification included reversing lamps, four-way hazard flashers, folding rear seat, wash-wipe for the windscreen, carpeting, cigarette lighter and a glove box with lock and light. An XL trim level came only with the plain 1600 engine and provided reclining backs to the front seats and carpet for the luggage compartment floor and centre console.

The GT. specification was available with 1600, 2000 and 3000 power units and was notable for the standard use of H4 halogen headlamps of higher wattage than had been offered previously on Capris, but remember we talk only of large rectangular lamps on the Capri II, rather than the more illuminating quadruple units provided on some Mark 1s and all Mark 3s. Also part of the GT specification were a clock, twin-tone horns and individually folding rear seats. Minor items included keying the colour of the

The automatic Ghia Capri II of 1974 demonstrates the split rear seat. Parochial observers of the British scene have observed that the Mini Metro drew inspiration from this source for its back seat layout, but it should be remembered that the Metro seats are of unequal squab width at the back.

carpets to the exterior of GT paintwork and two lamps in the tailgate luggage zone.

We have already discussed the Ghia model, but it should be recorded that the sports wheels, body coachline and rear screen wash-wipe, plus the extra-length bumper overriders and the interior map-reading lamp were all part of a sports custom pack — a faint reminder of the original X, XL and XLR options. One item that remained firmly on the option list for the initial Capri II production run was a luggage compartment load cover, causing a good deal of adverse press comment — another criticism that would not be fully answered throughout the range until the advent of the Mark 3.

Most of the items mentioned as standard equipment on the more expensive models could be purchased as individual options, including the sunroof, metallic paintwork (that of the Ghia had an extra lacquer layer) and halogen headlamps.

Running changes

Although it was over a year before any official changes were made to the model line, Ford took a considerable time in making both power steering and the 2-litre four-cylinder models freely available in all markets. Certainly Ford of Britain executives had power-steering 3-litre Ghias in 1974, the system proving light on first acquaintance, but accurate and sensitive enough for sporting drivers.

Separated rear exhausts came with 3-litre V6 in Britain, the Ghia offering its own eight-spoke alloy wheels, a vinyl roof, tinted glass and a sunroof amongst its standard features. The Capri 3.0 Ghia headed the 1974 range at just over £3,100.

Announced at the Geneva Show in March 1975, the all-black Capri S models were offered in a choice of 1600, 2000 (as seen here) and 3000 forms. The gold lining of the badgework and exterior panels was matched by gold cloth panels for the seats.

Sales began to drop during 1975 and Ford in Germany felt that the reason (based particularly on abrasive press comment) was that the car had lost its genuine sports appeal. It had become too soft, too much biased toward the family side of the schizophrenic character that the Capri has always had to offer to ensure commercial survival. Slowly, Cologne would influence the return of more sporting Capris. . . .

The Geneva Show in March 1975 had the forerunner of the Capri S on display. At first Ford showed this as the Midnight, in reference to the black colour scheme that pervaded every conceivable aspect of this Capri II, including the bumpers, door handles, glass surrounds and even the exhaust pipe! Inside, much of the same funereal theme was pursued, right down (or up, in this case) to the headlining. Contrasting with this 'black is beautiful' approach was the wide use of gold, or as near as they could get to that shade in the trim department, for the seat panels and gold side stripes for the body. This combination of black-and-gold was a subtle marketing/styling echo of the John Player colours which Lotus wore in Grand Prix racing, although without

the finely etched coachlines to emphasize basic panel shapes that were so popular amongst customizers seeking to copy the early-1970s Lotus decor.

Complete with tinted glass and gold-sprayed alloy wheels, the Germany-only Capri S models went on sale in Europe shortly after their show debut and were announced in the UK on June 10 that year. At first glance they might simply have been dismissed as carefully baited marketing traps, but underneath their snazzy paintwork there was a return to the harder spring rates of earlier Capris and the use of Bilstein gas dampers at the rear, mated to an appropriately firmer bump-and-rebound action from the conventional front struts. Anti-roll bars grew thicker and the Capri IIS, available with the usual 1600 OHC, 2000 OHC (or 2.3 V6 in Germany) and 3-litre V6, became a familiar sight on European roads. They also did much to restore the Capri's sporting credibility amongst European magazines, even the German press sounding happier about Ford's coupe.

In Britain the marketing men at Ford's Warley HQ decided to play it safe and offer the latest sporting Capris as Capri S GTs,

The seat inserts on the Capri S made a welcome contrast with the otherwise all-black interior, which even extended to the controls and the instrument surrounds as well as all the other exposed metalwork and plastic items.

but the GT tag was soon dropped as the move toward S was accepted by the customers. In June 1975 prices ranged from £2,330 for the 1600S to £2,543 for the 3000S. Gradually the Capri S became a full production model, following an initial special order and limited edition status. It remained recognizably the same car with the stiffer suspension and revised appearance, but there were distinct variations amongst the S-badged Capri IIs. Altogether three types of alloy wheel were fitted on the various models, including the Ghia nine-spoke alloy (from 1976 onwards in the UK), a similar multi-spoke design, but with four primary spokes defined (mainly on four-cylinder models of 1975-76) and the definitive four-spoke FAVO-Escort style of alloy that was on the first show cars and was recognized for international production racing (Group 1) from April 1976 for 3-litre Capris.

As they became popular and pricier (by 1977 the redesignated 3.0S cost £4,125) the Capri S-types appeared with many other standard production colours besides the original black. However, the gold side panel coachlines remained. More importantly a front spoiler, a glass-fibre addition to the lower panels, was incorporated during 1976. It was recognized for international

motor sport purposes from November that year, having been smoothly blended into the production panels of British Capri S models by the autumn, by which time the S also offered a three-spoke sports steering wheel — complete with crossed chequered flags in the centre! — and striped fabric inserts for the seats. The three-spoke steering wheel has remained in sportier Capris ever since, but carrying the comparatively sober company logo.

Marketing developments

Outside the Capri S introduction, the changes made during the 1974-78 life of the Capri II were mainly a marketing response to an increasing consumer awareness in Europe concerning the cost and equipment of cars made in the West as opposed to those of Japan. In other words, Ford had either to offer the Capri, along with other models in their range, with more equipment for the same price, or to reduce both the price and the equipment.

In October 1975 Ford of Britain took the initiative with their Value For Money (VFM) programme, a title and action which were to be echoed exactly by British Leyland in their autumn-1982 run up to the British Motor Show. Ford revitalized

By 1977 Capri S models had grown a front spoiler and with their firmer handling they represented a return to the Capri's more sporting origins. This particular Capri was modified by British Rallye Sport engineers for the author to test at Brands Hatch in triple Weber carburettor trim; the wheels are a 7in rim width derivative of the FAVO four-spoke design.

under the Ford coding Realignment Program, which had the effect of selling 10,000 Capris in the second half of 1976 instead of 8,000 recorded in the opening months of the year. In the same periods Britain took 19,000 and 17,000 Capri IIs, reflecting the fact that the car tended to be more widely accepted in the UK, where the VW Scirocco and GM Manta opposition was not so strongly established. Also in May 1976, the Germans got their 2-litre V6 alternative to the SOHC in-line four, the small six continuing to be a favourite in that country. The 1,999cc unit offered 90bhp at 5,000rpm and 110lb/ft of torque at 3,000rpm, which was sufficient for 106mph and 0-62mph in 13.3s, according to Ford figures.

By the summer of 1976 Capris were coming through in right-hand-drive form with the three-stalk steering column layout for lights, flashers and wipers that continued into the 1980s. Whereas facia-mounted switchgear used to operate the lamps, this move to the steering column allowed Ford to clean up the ergonomics a little with a central provision for up to four switches controlling refinements like the rear screen wash-wipe, heated rear screen (standard down to the cheapest 1300) and items that had started at extra cost but rapidly moved into the standard specification, such as rear fog warning lights. If you think this adds up to only three switches, note that the wiper action and the wash for the rear screen were sensibly divided so that one could just have the wiper on a wet day in traffic, rather than the compulsory dab of water that many current hatchbacks demand.

Despite the careful remedial marketing moves at Ford, the Capri II was soon dying on its feet, and when production of the American versions ceased in August 1977 the way was clear for a much more aggressive European-only Capri. After a production figure of 476,446 Capris made between January 1, 1974 and December 31, 1977 (Capri II commenced German full-scale production on January 1, 1974 and ceased on January 6, 1978) the 'Diana'-coded Capri II would make way for another Capri. But before we catch up on that newcomer, let's see how the Capri earned its sporting spurs. . . .

the Capri's appeal with the introduction of a base model at £116 under the 1300L's price tag. Equipment deleted included most of that which was simultaneously offered as standard within the upgraded 1300L — a marketing equipment trick *par excellence!* For example, an October 1975 Capri II 1300L offered cloth seats with reclining backs, a driver's door mirror and steel sports wheels. On the basic Capri II you stayed with the original fixed-back seats and rubber mats for the baggage compartment.

A new designation, GL, was the replacement for the previous XL and provided 1.6 and 2-litre models with a standard rear wash-wipe, halogen headlamps, the GT seats (which had slightly built-up squabs), a centre console and a clock. In May 1976 the Germans went in for a similar extra-value marketing exercise

CHAPTER 5

Capris in competition

Phase 1: 1969 to 1977

Following the competition trail blazed by Lotus Cortinas and Escort Twin-Cams, such an overtly sporting coupe as the Capri simply *had* to have a competition image to back up the sales talk. At first it was all about official Ford programmes based at the company's competition departments in Cologne (opened in January 1968) and at Boreham, in Essex, opened early in 1963. Ford of Britain had been competing since the 1950s with works cars prepared amongst press and American cars at Ford's Lincoln Cars building on London's Great West Road. Yet despite the intensive effort put into creating a genuine competition car of the 1969-74 Capri, the Capri II was left to the dedicated band of private racing teams in production car-based Group 1 events. There was one notable exception in the Boreham-prepared pair of Capri IIs that went racing at the Spa-Francorchamps 24-hours annual in July 1974, but otherwise the Capri II was left to outsiders. Why? Primarily because of events outside the small world of motor sports, but the Capri II itself, with its higher weight and a drag factor that was slightly up on the original (0.438 without the front spoiler for the Capri II 3000GT against 0.410 for the 1969 Capri 3000GT) certainly did not help to make the later Capri the natural competitor that the 1969-74 originals had become.

However, 'natural' was certainly not the right description for the first factory competition Capri. 'Inspired', or 'prophetic' would have been better descriptions of the mud-caked blue-and-white 3000GT which brought Ford of Britain's new coupe into millions of TV households on February 8, 1969, three days after sales began and little more than a week since the public preview of the Capri at the Brussels Motor Show.

To match the instant competition success notched up by the Escort after its 1968 announcement, Ford at Boreham knew they would have to do something pretty special to turn the Capri into a winner so quickly. The Escort had made its winning debut upon ITV's World of Sport Saturday afternoon coverage of the mixed-surface hybrid that is rallycross. I say the surfaces are mixed, but usually it is just the degree of slipperiness that varies, from diabolical to unprintable. The Escort made its mark by coupling modest dimensions and weight to at least 160bhp. Obviously the four-cylinder Capris that comprised the Capri launch stock were not man enough to match the power-to-weight ratio of an Escort Twin-Cam. Although it would have been technically possible to provide a Cosworth 16-valve engine of the type shown to and driven by the press, Ford at Boreham, under the managerial and inventive direction of former GP driver Henry Taylor, decided that the potential of the 3-litre V6 should be investigated. After all, the public would be getting a 3000GT the following autumn, but there was never much chance of a 'Capri RS1600' progressing further than a gambol amongst the Cypriot scenery for the edification of the Fourth Estate.

At this point the knowledgeable could snort into their beer and say, 'well, there wasn't much chance of the public getting their hands on a Four Wheel Drive (4-WD) Capri 3000GT, either,' for this was the combination Ford fielded to score a highly publicized rallycross victory in cold Croft that February! Yet Ford Advanced Vehicle Operations personnel most certainly did look sternly at a limited-production model, as the test-bay rollers to measure horsepower front and rear were still *in situ* when I joined FAVO in 1972. Rod Mansfield, as I write, head of the Special Vehicle

Engineering group at Dunton (the team which provided the Capri 2.8 Injection in 1981), told me that a serious development programme for the 4-WD road-going Capri was indeed undertaken in FAVO's early days, but 'it was killed by complexity in the end'.

Ford departments ordered at least 17 Capri 4-WDs for various tasks over the 1968-71 period, five of which were for competition purposes and the remainder part of those evaluation and development programmes that came to nought at the time. Yet Ford and Ferguson already knew more about the benefits of 4-WD than most of their rivals, for the production Mark 4 Zephyr 6 saloons had been extensively evaluated and endurance-tested in association with the British Police, allying the Borg-Warner 35 automatic transmission and the Capri's 2,994cc V6 engine with front and rear differentials of Zephyr independent rear suspension origin, and the Harry Ferguson Research Ltd's P134 4-WD central unit, the front differential running as an integral component within a new cast-alloy sump for the Ford V6. These prototypes mainly ran a 37 per cent front-wheel allocation of torque and 63 per cent rear. Some of the evaluation vehicles and one rallycross Capri tried the Dunlop-invented Maxaret anti-lock braking system as well — all this at least 12 years before the Audi Quattro made its Geneva Show debut in 1980.

As the first Capri preproduction machines trickled through to the Ford press department, Henry Taylor's team pirated a 1600GT and sent it to the Ferguson 4-WD specialists at Toll Bar, Coventry, in the autumn of 1968. By this stage Ferguson already had experience of 30 Zephyr V6 4-WD conversions and had supplied at least two Capris with V6 engines and 4-WD at the prototype price of £2,000 apiece for the conversion work. This involved 171lb of additional hardware (Audi talk these days of a meagre 30lb extra or so for 4-WD) and a total of 2,604lb (1,184kg) for the complete car in road-going trim. The conversion involved a Ferguson centre differential bolted to the tail of a five-speed ZF gearbox, the centre differential passing power forward via a shaft to the raised engine, or more correctly to the sump and forward differential beneath the V6, the forward drive-shaft actually passing through the deepest part of the engine oil sump pan.

The first competition 4-WD Capri was primarily the responsibility of Ferguson, but later Ford at Boreham took on the majority of the 4-WD installation work, as well as the Weslake-modified V6, which provided a quoted 160bhp with its high-performance camshaft and gas-flowed cylinder heads. The versatile Boreham mechanics hacked out a competition Capri in weeks using their own 12-gauge steel tubing to replace the production engine frame and cutting away the front chassis rails to accommodate the new drive-shafts to the front wheels. Then Boreham's men made up new engine mounts, located the front struts with a top mounting point raised some 1¾in, and incorporated the front-drive uprights of the German Taunus, amongst many other tasks.

As already noted, that first rallycross Capri was an instant success, but Roger Clark only drove it once before the whole works effort shifted from the Capri to preparation of the pushrod Escort fleet that had to tackle the 1970 London-Mexico marathon rally (which Hannu Mikkola duly won). Late 1970 and the early months of 1971 were spent preparing three new rallycross 3-litre Capris with the Ferguson 4-WD system and more powerful engines.

Driven by Roger and Stan Clark, with the third example appearing somewhat belatedly just before Christmas 1970 for rallycross specialist Rod Chapman, the Capri trio shook the ground, shifted earth at a rate that Chapman — a demolition contractor — envied and conquered the results sheets of the Castrol-financed Cadwell Park Championship televised by ITV. Roger Clark collected the title after a record-breaking spree of front drive-shaft failures caused by the necessarily extensive front wheel movement. The BBC series at Lydden Hill was also attacked by the Capris, but here the penalties imposed by the organizers — starting at least 10s behind the two-wheel-driven cars and having to make up the deficit through lakes of mud in three swift laps — were enough to ensure the works Fords generally provided spectacle rather than outright victories.

These 1970-71 Capris featured Bilstein damping, an extra leaf spring on each side of the production rear axle, heavy-duty bushes for the standard rear axle links and Ferodo equipment for the ordinary disc-drum layout. Maximum speeds at Lydden could be as high as 90mph, but at Cadwell Park an independent radar gun established speeds between 72 and 68mph. Times compared to an Escort? When I attended that December 1970 Cadwell Championship meeting Roger Clark's best practice lap was 1m 1.6s, compared with John Taylor's 1m 6.0s in a 1.8-litre pushrod

Mick Jones and Roger Clark contemplate the one-off engine of the four-wheel-drive Capri built for the latter to drive in rallycross. Those ram stacks and the Lucas mechanical fuel injection fed the Weslake-headed V6 to produce a power output reported to be in excess of 250bhp. Also evident are the raised front strut mountings.

version, so the 4-WD message was clear even then!

The V6 engines were interesting as the result of a Ford-Weslake development programme, though they had nothing to do with the Cologne-based Capri racing programme we shall discuss shortly, being entirely based on the British 'Essex' 2,994cc unit. They started off with a series of milder head and camshaft modifications that later provided the basis for a widely marketed series of road performance kits under the Weslake name, but by late-1970 Boreham and Weslake were on to a racing spec with compression ratios in excess of 11.2:1, larger inlet and exhaust valves and two choices of fuel-injection system to feed the six cylinders. More common was the Tecalemit-Jackson continuous system. But for Roger Clark they managed to salvage two aluminium alloy cylinder heads from a very expensive development programme, V6 versions of the Gurney Weslake alloy heads successfully used on the V8 engine of the Ford GT40, complete

In 1970 Ford and Weslake developed a 2.4-litre version of the Capri 2300GT for European Touring Car Championship events. A lot of retirements were suffered, including an engine failure for this Rolf Stommelen-driven Capri during the September 1970 Silverstone Tourist Trophy; team-mates Manfred Mohr/ Dieter Glemser were fifth, while a third Capri also broke its engine. It is interesting to see how the front spoiler developed around the grilled twin oil coolers; pop-rivetting of the wheelarches was crude by later standards.

with enormous valves. These were mated with an awesome Lucas mechanical injection system — 'awesome' because it hid beneath an oversize bonnet bulge necessitated by using CanAm-style ram trumpets on the intakes above the system.

Whereas the Tecalemit-injected engines were said to deliver around 210-220bhp, the Lucas demon motor (which was bored 0.60 thous oversize *à la* RS3100) was credited with 252bhp at 6,100rpm.

Boreham bow out

The TV companies and the large car manufacturers soon lost interest in rallycross as a sport to occupy peak sporting time regularly and Ford at Boreham shifted ever more into their phenomenally successful Escort RS1600 rallying activities, winning all but the Monte Carlo Rally with almost monotonous regularity until their retirement from any kind of official works competition in 1979. However, the Essex airfield site did provide

a 1970 Cologne specification Capri for Gerry Birrell to race in the 1971 British Saloon Car Championship and this car collected two wins, a second and a fourth place.

Ford at Boreham fielded Group 1 production Capris with very few modifications for the 1973 Avon Motor Tour of Britain and backed the start of production saloon car racing in the 1972 British season by letting three Group 1 3000GTs out for Dave Brodie and David Matthews, and Ford protégé Gillian Fortescue-Thomas. As these ventures failed to produce the kind of success that the rally Escorts delivered in world-class events, there was an understandable lack of enthusiasm for a class of racing based on comparatively unmodified cars, whereas both the rally Escorts and the continental racing Capris were radically re-engineered in every fundamental respect.

For the record, the Capri 3-litre team on the Tour of Britain utilized Roger Clark, Dave Matthews and Prince Michael of Kent as drivers, but all were beaten by Gordon Spice's works-

The 1970 East African Safari assault by three Capris failed utterly after the inspiration of an unexpected 1969 victory by a Taunus V6 saloon.

loaned earlier 3000GT — and James Hunt won the event in a Chevrolet Camaro 5.7-litre V8. In the circuit races of 1972 Matthews and Brodie scored eight outright victories apiece, but again the Chevrolet Camaro was beginning to draw ahead into a class of its own by the close of the season. Ford tried using the Mustang to crack this GM problem, but after Boreham-contracted Gerry Birrell crashed the beast heavily in testing at Snetterton no more was heard of that project!

More successful, following the tragic 1973 death of the highly talented Gerry Birrell, was the 1974 employment of Tom Walkinshaw in one of the ex-Tour of Britain Capris to fight for the 3-litre class of the reconstituted Group 1 British Saloon Car Championship. Against first-class opposition from Opel and BMW the Capri gradually got the upper hand with the aid of close to 180bhp. It won its class, but Chevrolets were destined to carry on winning overall until a 3-litre capacity limit was installed for the 1976 season. By this time, Ford at Boreham seemed thoroughly bored with saloon car racing and — with the exception of that unsuccessful sortie to Spa in 1974 with Capri IIs for John Fitzpatrick and Tom Walkinshaw — they tended to leave racing and Capri development to British privateers in Group 1 production events, and to the German factory and their eager consorts at Zakspeed in the classes that demanded more engineering finesse — the Group 2 European Touring Car Championship and the Group 5 German National Championship.

Rally red herring

Germany's fledgling department in Cologne began with 1968 sorties in racing using all kinds of Escorts and talent such as that of Rolf Stommelen, but by November they had accrued enough experience with the Taunus 20M RS (which used the same 2.3-litre V6 as the Capri) to set out on the London-Sydney Marathon with a trio of these cars. It was a tall spares and fuel administration order for such a young team, but they held the lead at one point and challenged Roger Clark/Ove Andersson's Boreham Cortina for leadership across Europe with their Taunus crewed by Simo Lampinen/Gilbert Staepelaere. Although crashes in Australia eventually demoted them to seventh and sixteenth overall with their two surviving cars, the team's basic ability and the effectiveness of their liaison with Weslake in Britain, that had produced 150bhp with good tractability, encouraged more ambitious outings.

Such optimism led to a rather large 'red herring' trail in the Capri's competition life, for Ford in Cologne actually went out and won the 1969 East African Safari Rally outright. The immediate and unexpected success of Robin Hillyar/Jock Aird in the comparatively bulky Taunus saloon led Jochen Neerpasch,

The Spa-Francorchamps 24-hours race in 1971 provided the first of five victories scored by Capris in the annual Belgian classic. Two of the successes came from the works team, including a 1-2-3 in 1972, and three from Gordon Spice Racing with Mark 3 cars (in 1978-80). Here is Dieter Glemser shortly after the start in the car he shared to victory with the Spaniard Alex Soler-Roig at an average speed of 113.51mph.

Martin Braungart and Michael Kranefuss at Cologne up an expensive rallying blind alley.

Following that 1969 Safari win and a limited programme of tarmac events that included the debut of Weslake-Cologne Capris on France's Lyons-Charbonnières rally, Ford's German sporting administration decided they would go racing *and* rallying in 1970 with their Capri V6s! In 1969 they had used Capris in 170bhp triple-Solex-carburated 2.3-litre guise to finish fourth (Dieter Glemser/Klaus Kaiser) and seventh on that inaugural French rally, then predominantly suffered retirements on the August Marathon de la Route and Tour de France (Jean-Francois Piot was the only works Capri finisher for a class win and sixth overall). However, they had been steadily developing the car for fast tarmac work, Weslake progressing from a carburated 2,293cc V6 to the use of Lucas fuel-injection on the same power unit by the time of the Tour de France (giving 190bhp at 7,200rpm). By the end of the season they had also prepared a prototype 2600GT to provide similar power, but at lower crankshaft rpm — the first 2.6-litre provided 190bhp at 6,000rpm, running the same injection and a 10.5:1 compression ratio. This Capri 2600GT

also provided the marque's best 1969 result, recording a third overall for Jean-Francois Piot and 1981 Talbot Competition Director Jean Todt in the tough Mediterranean island road race known as the Tour de Corse.

1970: 'A complete disaster'

The Kugelfischer injection system and the Capri 2300GT were selected as the armoury with which Ford would attack 1970, but the results were, in Michael Kranefuss' concise comment, 'a complete disaster for us'. In nine rounds of the European Championship the 2,397cc over-bored V6s were equipped with Weslake aluminium cylinder heads and mothered ceaselessly by both Weslake and former BMW engineer Otto Stulle, yet they blew up with disturbing regularity. There was an encouraging second place at the opening Monza round and a similar result in Budapest, but the humiliation of three engine failures on their 'home' Nurburgring six-hours race and the elimination of both works Capris from the final Spanish round ensured that they would seek outside help for 1971.

The Safari story was no better. Not one of the three 190bhp

The 1971 European Championship season ended on the Jarama circuit in Spain with a fraught event for Dieter Glemser, who had to overcome a throttle linkage malady in order to finish third and take the driver's title.

injected 2300GTs made the finish, although Rauno Aaltonen/Peter Huth proved that the five-speed ZF-equipped Ford with its lightweight panels was certainly fast enough to do the job over the early stages. There would be no more works Capris prepared for rallying after a public debacle that was all too clearly recorded by the Ford press department's journalistic guests!

Meanwhile, throughout the 1970 season the Capri had begun its growth on the tracks from tuned saloon car to purpose-built racer. The wheel widths grew rapidly, Tech Del Minilites replaced by Limmer-branded designs with cast-alloy centre and spun aluminium rim (very similar to the present day BBS, a company which now takes up all Martin Braungart's working hours). As the wheels grew, so great sections of the body were hacked away and pop-rivetted lightweight panels popped into their place. At the front the spoilers first grew up around the twin oil coolers and then developed into full-width aerodynamic devices.

By 1971 Braungart and the team had learned the lessons of the racing Escorts and had installed completely new MacPherson front struts with proper location arms, a process repeated at the rear by long top and bottom radius links, vertical coil spring/damper units above the back axle and just the vestigial remains of a leaf spring (some were in plastic!) to comply with the Group 2 regulations. Over the seasons that the Capri was raced in modified form the details changed, massive ventilated four-wheel discs growing at the same pace as Limmer and Dunlop were able to progress from 13in standard wheel diameter to 16in, holding rims up to 14in wide by 1973. Dunlop offered progressively lower and wider tyre profiles and sections and the whole assembly had to be covered by increasingly more sophisticated glass-fibre wheelarch extensions, which actually stretched from nose to tail and just ignored the doors in the search for width!

Yet, as they prepared for 1971 with their sophisticated chassis ('the first real racing saloon made in Germany', as one BMW man revealed) there was still the V6 engine headache. At this point former Boreham engine builder Peter Ashcroft was assigned to a six-month Cologne troubleshooting mission. Working alongside Braungart, the blunt practicality of the Lancastrian destined to be Ford's next British Competition Manager after Stuart Turner, plus the hardworking engineering skills of former Mercedes man Braungart, produced much of the 'Escortization' that was needed

for reliable race-winning performance. Ashcroft amazed the Germans with his cheerful defiance of company rules (Braungart always tracked him down in the workshops by looking for the plumes of smoke emitting from Peter's illicit cigarettes smouldering beneath the *Rauchen Verboten* signs!) and by calling Keith Duckworth in Britain to ask for advice. It materialized that the crankshaft design was fundamentally wrong for a high-revving race engine, the V6 literally shaking itself apart at the 7,000rpm and more that was demanded. Not only was the crankshaft redesigned and a new steel one manufactured by co-operative work at Weslake, but the iron cylinder block was strengthened (the basic design went on to be used for the 2.8-litre 'Arizona' series production V6). Steel connecting rods, new pistons and a dry-sump lubrication system were concocted, all this work drawing on proven competition practice, though there were of course problems peculiar to racing a V6 engine that had not been encountered in previous Fords.

The RS2600 had been homologated on October 1, 1970, so they had a much better base for 1971 competitions, beginning the season with 2,873cc and 265bhp at 7,300rpm. This involved the usual production RS stroke of 69mm that had to be retained under the regulations, plus a bore size of 94mm. Although the Kugelfischer mechanical injection remained a feature through the racing life of the RS2600, the compression ratio crept up from an initial 10.5:1 to 11:1 by the close of 1971 and eventually 11.3:1 two years later, by which time the absolute maximum of 325bhp from a 2,995cc stretch of the same basic engine (96mm × 69mm) was obtained at the somewhat ragged edge of the V6's reliability. On the road it provided 150bhp and plenty of 120mph thrills, but the wheel-lifting racers with their 160mph-plus capabilities were something else again.

1971-72: The dominant years

Although the winter work of the Anglo-German collaborators covered virtually every aspect of the V6, a weakness materialized in the head gaskets for the first race of 1971. This resulted in a retirement for Dieter Glemser and the Spaniard Alex Soler-Roig, but only after they had set new records and led over half the opening Monza four-hours European Championship qualifying event. Thereafter Lechler sealing rings were sunk inside the main gaskets and located directly into grooves in the top of the now

The 1972 European Championship season opened at Monza with a win for Gerard Larrousse (later to become Renault's Competition Director) and Jochen Mass. However, the works Capris were opposed by the silver Schnitzer BMW coupe, seen here in second place and destined to beat the Fords at the Nurburgring.

Cutaway of the 1972 racing Capri revealing the four-wheel ventilated disc brakes, the fuel-injection engine of nearly 3 litres and the multiple links to locate the rear axle. Dry-sump lubrication equipment and the safety racing fuel tank dominated the boot.

Earlier version of the 2.9-litre Ford-Weslake racing V6 with its vertical fuel-injection stacks and rubber belt drives to the alternator and, on the right, the fuel-injection metering unit.

A gaggle of limited-edition Capri 3000Es pound around the infamous Paddock Hill Bend during a celebrity race at a Brands Hatch Ford Sport day in 1972. Preparation of the cars by fitting the regulation safety equipment was carried out by John Young's Super Speed team in Ilford.

Gerry Birrell at Paul Ricard in 1972, displaying the style that had taken him to fastest practice time and second place overall the previous year. This time he was to be out of luck and Brian Muir/John Miles won the event in a Capri run in Wiggins Teape colours for the 1972 British Championship. This Frami Racing/Kent Capri has now been sold to TWR for restoration.

stronger cylinder block.

Thereafter the Capris simply smashed any vestige of opposition in the big class, so much so that Neerpasch, Braungart and driver Hans-Joachim Stuck all defected to BMW in order to provide a 1973 challenge for the all-conquering Capris they had helped to become such monotonous winners. The Capri record in 1971 European Championship events was outright victory in six of eight rounds, including a 1-2-3 finish in the Austrian Salzburgring event that marked the team's first outright success. Rose grower and former Mercedes rallyist Dieter Glemser took the title of European Champion driver while six victories in the German Championship brought Michael Kranefuss' protégé Jochen Mass the National title. However, Ford failed to win the European title for marques, which went to Alfa Romeo as a result of their efforts in the 1300cc class.

In 1972 it was more of the success recipe with eight wins in nine European rounds — they were only beaten at the Nurburgring, but that July day was a painful reminder that Neerpasch had left. A private Schnitzer BMW coupe with former Ford driver John Fitzpatrick on the strength and Neerpasch in the pits 'on the other side' beat the Fords on home territory. Jochen Mass took the European drivers' title, Hans-Joachim Stuck the German Championship (with nine victories) and the

Capri RS2600 also won the Belgian National title and the Finnish Ice Racing Championship, the latter by courtesy of Timo Makinen. A man who was not scared by an Austin-Healey 3000 hardly noticed the Capri's wayward mannerisms with nearly 300bhp spurting from the studded rear wheels!

At the close of 1972 the works Capri RS2600s had won races all over Europe, had finished Le Mans eighth and tenth, had performed well enough to net Ford and Jochen Mass the manufacturers' title in the South African Springbok series, and had even won a race in Macao. Independent tests established that with 290bhp at 7,500rpm the now blue-and-white factory Fords (a colour scheme adopted in August 1971) were capable not only of reaching 163mph at Le Mans or Spa, but also of leaping from rest to 62mph in a scant 4.6s; 0-124mph took some 4 seconds less than a Capri 1300 occupied in reaching 60mph from rest.

Along came BMW

As explained in the RS2600/RS3100 chapter, Ford were not only feeling the loss of such key personnel as Neerpasch, Braungart and Stuck, but also the lack of aerodynamic devices in 1973. At first the contest with the revitalized BMW team (which was assisted by two very able privateer teams) was fairly even in the European Championship, Ford winning two of the first three

The story of 1973! Ford versus BMW at Silverstone. Once the BMWs had got their wings only the stunning driving of Jochen Mass could keep the Capri in touch. Mass managed a magnificent second place at Silverstone and equalled the lap record time of Stuck's BMW, this in a car with some 50bhp less and without a rear wing!

John Fitzpatrick three-wheels the 160mph racing Capri to an easy victory at the Salzburgring in spring 1973, one of only two wins scored in eight European Championship rounds that year.

rounds with Capris that had revised exterior aerodynamics (but no rear spoiler) and drivers such as Jackie Stewart and Jody Scheckter.

However, in July 1973 the tide turned irreversibly against Ford when Braungart conceived and rushed to production and homologation a multi-piece set of wings, strakes and hoops that simply put the BMW CSLs beyond reach of even the heroics of Jochen Mass in the latest 320bhp works Ford. From July onwards the Ford team failed to win another European Championship race — although there were some epic confrontations when sheer bravery and brawn from Mass nearly overcame BMW brains. Gone were the chances of either the European or the German title.

High hopes were placed on a recovery in 1974, when Cosworth's work on a four-valve-per-cylinder version of the British 'Essex' V6 would yield over 400bhp and a tail spoiler would be part of the specification, thanks to the appearance of the Ford Capri RS3100. New driving talent was recruited, too, including BMW's 1973 Champion Toine Hezemans and former BMW Alpina driver Niki Lauda.

The new RS3100s were certainly more powerful, their Lucas (and later Kugelfischer) injected 3,412cc V6s providing from 415 to 455bhp as the seasons progressed, but the Capris were also heavier (2,288lb/1,040kg) and found themselves in a world where the price and availability of petrol had become a prior concern to that of beating the Bavarians.

The 1973 cockpit for the racing Capri; at many qualifying rounds the scrutineers insisted on passenger seat fitment.

The works RS3100s did race, scoring their first win at the August 1974 European Championship round at Zandvoort after a season in which both BMW and Ford tended to miss more races than those they actually contested. The most powerful Group 2 Capris appeared occasionally even after the Cologne Competition Department was officially shut — increasing the emphasis on outside sponsorship and outfits like Zakspeed, who won for Ford the 1974 European Championship with their nimble 2-litre RS Escorts. The last race I have on record for a factory RS3100 was almost a year after the department in Germany was closed — Jochen Mass and Klaus Ludwig retiring from the November 1975 Kyalami 1,000-kilometres event. However, that was not the end of the Capri's works-backed exploits, as we shall see in a later chapter.

Backing Britain

In Britain the pattern of Ford at Boreham loaning out complete Capris was replaced by the supply of bare shells and other important basic parts as the privateers became more and more successful with Capri II. Former Weslake engineer John Griffiths, now working at Boreham, ensured that the Ford 3-litre remained a jump ahead of the opposition, homologating items

Silverstone, September 1973, and John Fitzpatrick exhibits the guts all team drivers had to display in order to counteract BMW's wing advantage. John remembers this two-wheeling device as one of the most difficult cars he has ever driven in a career spanning more than 20 years.

Mike Hall, at Cosworth Engineering in Northampton, drew up this belt-driven quadruple overhead-camshaft version of the British 'Essex' Ford V6 engine for the 1974 season. The GAA engine contained the traditional and unmatched Cosworth four-valve-per-cylinder combustion chambers and developed over 400bhp from 3.4 litres. Later, the power plant found some success in British Formula 5000 single-seater racing, but the fuel crisis robbed us of frequent appearances for such monstrous Group 2 Capris.

Ford Cologne started with a very basic body for the 1973 team cars. Contrast the neat glass-fibre wheelarch extensions with those of the 1970 team cars shown earlier.

At the Nurburgring, in July 1974, the Capri RS3100s and big BMWs fought such a battle that an Escort won! Here we can admire the superb 1974 rendition of the traditional blue-and-white livery, colours that succeeded the original silver-and-blue finish during the 1971 season.

that increased engine power (higher compression, bigger valves and a new camshaft amongst them) as well as a gearbox with Hewland close ratios and 9.75in diameter front disc brakes in the years 1976-77. Perhaps the cleverest step was ensuring that the Capri II was recognized as an evolution of the original, thereby keeping the light weight that has been such an essential part of its competition success.

Tom Walkinshaw provided much of the initial impetus to keep the Capri competitive before he relinquished his Boreham retainer at the end of 1976, yet the main success for the model came from Staines-based accessory magnate Gordon Spice, who provided a string of outright wins and top-capacity class titles in championships from 1975-80. Throughout these years he used 3-litre Capris prepared by CC Racing, at Kirbymoorside (their 200-220bhp V6s prepared by Neil Brown at Spalding, Lincolnshire), with a distinct performance and results boost when 'Capri III' appeared in 1978. However, this and the story of the most powerful and best-handling Capris ever (complete with limited ground effects), must wait while we explore the third (and last) generation of the production model.

Salzburgring in 1974, and one of two works Capris makes its debut in RS3100 winged form, with side radiators. Both cars, driven by 1973 European Champion Toine Hezemans, shown here, and team mate Niki Lauda, failed to finish. Why? Hezemans told his former employers at BMW, 'I have two engines in my Capri,' a reference to the V6 block which had split in half!

A show of Capri strength in Germany. Rolf Stommelen leads Toine Hezemans to a fine 1-2 victory in the 1974 national Eifelrennen held at the Nurburgring.

Tom Walkinshaw and John Fitzpatrick shared this Capri II for the 1974 Spa 24-hour race. They qualified second fastest and led for several hours, but lost a rear wheel and halfshaft. This and a sister car built for BP Belgium were passed on to a Hermetite-sponsored team for 1975. These were the last works racing Capris built by Ford at Boreham.

Vince Woodman and John Buncombe, two Ford dealers from the West Country, shared many of Vince's racing Capris in long-distance events, particularly at Spa-Francorchamps. Here, revealing the scars of battle, they show the grit that took them to so many finishes, running the Esso Capri II in the European Touring Car Championship round at Brands Hatch in 1978. Woodman went on to become Britain's most successful Capri driver in 1982.

CHAPTER 6

The third generation: 1978 to 1986

Refinement and development

On March 2, 1978 at a Ford press briefing, the latest Capri, coded as 'Carla', was launched with such gems as 'Ford engineers have achieved a major service breakthrough with the third-generation Capri' and 'the product of a young team of Ford engineers and designers who just cannot keep their hands off the car' and even 'two years of concentrated aerodynamic research have resulted in an even sleeker appearance and an altogether faster, safer and even more economical car. Smart new interior designs and engineering changes that reduce servicing and lower ownership costs are other bonuses.'

Yes, the Capri had changed for the better, but it was very much a question of running changes rather than a brand new model to face up to the increasing competition from front-wheel-drive small coupes, which were steadily eroding Capri sales to the point where 1981 production amounted to only 34,658 units. Putting this in a Ford perspective, only just over 7,000 more Capris were to be made in a year than the number of Escorts sold in Britain during the month of August 1982. Long gone were the days of the Capri appearing in the top-10 sellers; approximately 22,000 Capris were sold in the UK during 1981 and less than 20,000 in 1982.

However, Ford obviously found it worthwhile to incorporate some useful changes in the Capri format, modifications that really amounted to giving the Capri II a crisper look with some easily absorbed panel changes. It is an easy matter to change a Capri II's appearance into that of a 'Capri III', which is exactly what many Capri racers did in 1978. All you need is the money for and access to the following items: 'Capri III' wings, bonnet, lower valance (with built-in spoiler), quadruple 5¾in headlamps and revised tail-light clusters. Wrapround bumpers, largely the black-finished units of before with plastic extensions, plus the louvred grille that had been successfully exploited on the Fiesta were included on all models, as were integral fog warning lights within the rear lights, the ridging of which was an echo of Mercedes practice that Ford were to adopt across their range (except the Fiesta) by the time the Granada was revised in the summer of 1981.

As with the front-wheel-drive Ford Escort launched in 1980, Ford made a big play over the drag coefficient (Cd) of the revised Capri. With the tail spoiler, offered as standard on the S-models, they reckoned that its coefficient of 0.374 represented a 12.6 per cent improvement over the original Capri II GT and that in 3-litre form the new car had a top speed of around 124mph. They assessed the unspoilered lesser models, which now had a front air dam neatly incorporated beneath their lower front valance, as having a Cd figure of 0.403. In the May 29 issue of *Autocar,* John Miles revealed that the computerized readout at the MIRA wind-tunnel displayed a 0.414 Cd for his 'unmodified' 3.2-litre Capri S; after nine detail modifications, including a completely new spoiler of deeper design with a specially modified leading edge, wheel trims and a smaller ducktail rear spoiler, he reported a reduction in the Cd figure to 0.375. Regardless of the variance in the MIRA and the publicized drag factors, it was clear that with the latest Capri the customer was getting a better deal than before.

The louvred grille was composed of individual miniaturized aerofoil-section blades. Ford explained that because the area of the grille was about 10 per cent of that of the total vehicle, an improvement of 1.5 per cent in overall wind resistance was being

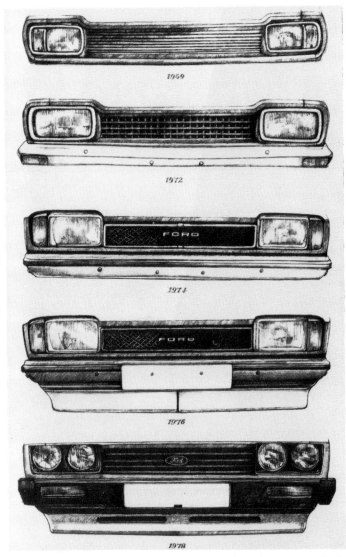

1969

1972

1974

1976

1978

A multiple sketch showing how the changing Capri face was gradually bearded with integral spoilers.

achieved by the use of the grille 'aerofoils'.

Their next development project was the design of various front-end spoilers and a comparison of these with the front-end device that had been added during the life of the Capri II. 'This proved so effective that it was introduced into production in the middle of 1975 as part of the Capri S specification. By this means total drag was reduced by 7 per cent and lift by 6 per cent', Ford said. Independent research and practical motorway experience have regularly shown front-end lift to be the big problem with the earlier Capris, which is why the front end should always be set to ride significantly lower than the back for road use. Ford attributed the integrated spoiler, louvred grille and reshaped bonnet — which joined the wing panel work in providing a drooping eyelid effect over the lamps and had a new line in phallic bonnet contours — with an overall 6 per cent reduction in Cd and a reduction of 18 per cent in front-end lift.

At the rear, Ford figures showed that a dramatic 60 per cent reduction in rear-end lift was possible with the S-spoiler and 'a further 5 per cent drag reduction'. Figures within FAVO revealed that a Capri II equipped with a rear spoiler could just slip beneath the 0.40 barrier, so I would never scoff at the private Capri II owner who fitted spoilers patterned on the works front and rear layouts. It should help not only to steady the car in crosswinds but also to provide a noticeable top-speed bonus.

Servicing extension

Welcome though the aerodynamic and associated minor styling changes may have been (especially the overdue incorporation of a rigid parcels shelf/luggage area cover for all models of GL specification and above), the private Capri owner and particularly the fleet manager welcomed the extended service intervals. Ford said at the time that the provision of 12,000-mile standard service intervals with an interim service at 6,000 miles 'makes the Capri less expensive to maintain over 20,000 miles than any other car in its class'. Ford oil change intervals had been every 6,000 miles from the start of Capri production, but the company pointed to 'lubricated for life' transmission, rear axle, steering rack and all suspension joints, plus 'fully self-adjusting brakes with lining wear inspection apertures in the rear back plates', as part of the reduced servicing need which was '44 per cent down over 20,000 miles' compared with the previous Capri. Certainly it was a lot

The third major Capri model came in March 1978 and exhibited aerodynamic alterations to the sheet metal on the same floorpan and mechanical base as has served the Ford since 1974. However, many detail modifications were also made to help both service cost and accident repair price reduction, including multi-piece bumpers, a plastic grille and other uses of plastics, both deformable and rigid, to reduce weight as well as help deflect the odd minor bump. Biggest plus points for the average motorist in the lower level models were the improved lighting and the standard use of laminated windscreen glass.

easier to inspect fluid levels for the brakes, the battery and the screen washers, while a general tidying of the underbonnet area meant that a blown fuse could be located or an accessory fitted a lot faster than used to be the case. Valve gear adjustment intervals were also doubled on all models apart from the 3-litre.

Equipment and model range

The engine and transmission line remained much as before, but there were minor changes in quoted horsepower for some markets. Ford of Britain talked of a gain from 50 to 57bhp for the same 9.2:1-compression 1,298cc crossflow unit that had always

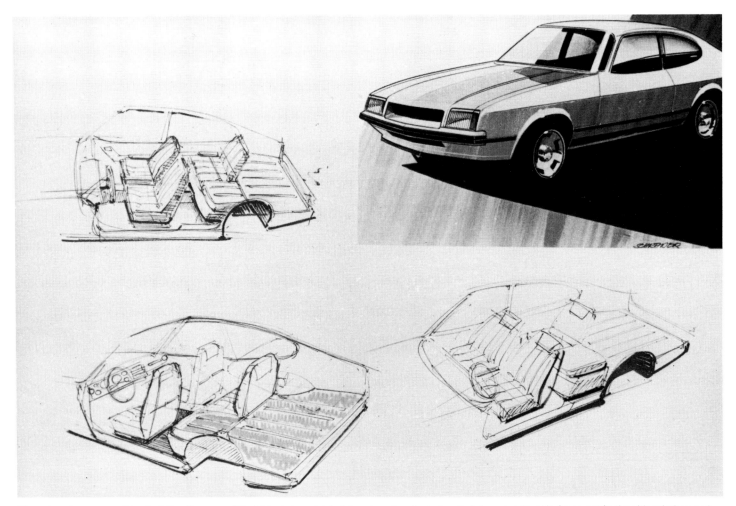

They almost gave us a Vauxhall Cavalier coupe/Opel Manta by mistake! A series of early design sketches reveals a desire to retain the side window and windscreen line of the earlier body.

been used, although the higher figure had been quoted for some years prior to that date, following the uprating process we noted in the chapter concerning the 1969 Capri. The German works offered a 1.3 with either 54bhp from an 8:1 cr version of that engine or 57bhp with a 9.2:1 compression.

Thus the UK 'third generation' Capris comprised the following models: A 1300 with 57bhp for £2,792 and an L version of the same car at £2,928. Then came the 1600L and GL with 72bhp at

£3,101 and £3,362, respectively. The uprated — formerly GT — 1600 SOHC engine of the 1600S continued to offer 88bhp, but the price had grown to £3,822. At 2 litres you could choose between the softer 2000GL at £3,560 or the 2000S for £3,940; both had the 98bhp SOHC engine of Pinto/Cortina ancestry. There was also another 2-litre choice, the Ghia at £4,697. The 3-litre Capri buyer was offered either a Ghia at £5,337 with standard automatic transmission (which was an extra throughout the rest of the range at £253) or the 3000S for £4,327. Power output was now quoted at 138bhp DIN in each case.

Prices had increased alarmingly since the original Capri's birth, but so had those of nearly all new cars on the British market, sales of which had been propped up by the growing business market which has become such a strong feature of British new car registrations and a particularly important aspect of Ford sales. Yet put in proper context, a 3000S still offered the most remarkable value-per-£-spent. *Autocar's* test of a 3000S revealed a 118mph maximum allied to 19.5mpg overall fuel consumption (including flat-out performance testing) and a formidable 8.6s capability from rest to 60mph. This made the 3000S some 5mph slower than the 4.2 manual Jaguar XJ6, a tenth of a second *quicker* to 60mph and 3.5mpg more economical, besides which the Jaguar then cost £9,753. Even the £10,171 Lotus Esprit was not much quicker at 124mph and 0-60mph in 8.4s. However, even the most devout Capri enthusiast should acknowledge that a mid-engined Lotus is likely to scuttle around corners faster and have better brakes than a conventional steel-bodied saloon!

Externally the new Capris carried the previous S matt black theme further than before for lesser models. Such a finish was applied to window surrounds, door handles, mirrors and bumpers and Capris with a radio aerial even had their antenna sprayed black! More useful was the L, GL and Ghia heavy rubber side moulding that prevented most car park dents. The sides of the S marked a new high in ostentation for Ford with an enormous 'S' decal and striping, which were astonishingly expensive to replace should the vehicle suffer a minor traffic accident. Incidentally, only Ghia and GL models had the rear fog lamps as standard, the others merely having space for them in the rear lamp cluster, and only GL, Ghia and S versions had the package tray in their standard specification.

More important to the enthusiast sifting through the catalogue

S, GL and Ghia models were all given a rear shelf as standard equipment, more useful for hiding boot contents from avaricious eyes than for putting anything on. Ridging of the rear lights became a Ford trademark in the early 1980s.

was the spread of gas damping for the rear telescopic units down to all but the base models, along with the smaller three-spoke steering wheel that had originated on the S (and prior to that on RS Escorts) and halogen headlamps for the quad front layout. The latter finally removed any qualms over the Capri's lighting standards throughout the range. Also standard at all levels — and about time, too — were laminated front screens. Those with an eye for detail may care to note that it was at this point that the basic facelifted facia of the 1972 Capri acquired some padding, while the instruments wore orange needles.

On the options list there were some important new items. For the S-owner there was alternative Recaro front seating of a semi-

The 1978 Capri S — seen here on test in France — stood on Ghia wheels and gained a soft plastic rear spoiler along with a giant side stripe and positively loud seat trim. Recaro seats were a desirable option in the opinion of most testers.

bucket style that most hard drivers adore, but which should be checked carefully by those with any inclination toward back pains because the backrest padding can be a little mean; it is easy enough to add extra padding, if required. Originally, Recaros were a £75.84 option. Also on the options list were powerful spray jet headlamp washers (£56.14), which worked well so long as dirt had not dried on the lamp lenses, while other useful extras were a remote-control driver's door mirror (£22.70), which

operated via a rather primitive selection of wires and lense adjusters, and the simply superb steel sunroof (then £146), which offered a tilt position as well as winding back to add a fine fresh-air dimension to Capri motoring.

Performance

Engines for the German market remained as they had been for later Capri IIs, but Ford amended their performance claims

The GL was instantly distinguished from a plain L by chrome-ringed sports road wheels in steel. It had a good value standard equipment list with rear gas dampers, four halogen lamps and a cloth interior of excellent comfort for the front seat occupants. The passenger's side rear-view mirror was added to the list in 1979.

Metallic paint, stereo radio and cassette player and inertia reel seat belts were included in the unaltered total price of the Capri Ghias. Note the headlamp washer jets and the increasing use of matt black paint to frame the windows at the side and finish both mirror and wipers.

Ford used the visit of the USAC racers in 1978 as a handy excuse to prepare a Rallye Sport Capri demonstrator with the enlarged wheelarches, deeper front spoiler and wide wheels that were still very popular buys from RS dealers in the early 1980s. Similar equipment was offered under the X-pack scheme. However, only extrovert law-breakers went for the full flashing roof light kit!

throughout Europe to take account of the revised shape and largely unchanged body weights. These now ranged from 87mph and 0-60mph in 20s for the 1300 to 122mph and 8.5s attributed to the 3-litre versions. In between, the models most likely to interest British enthusiasts included the 104mph 1600S, with a 13.5s 0-60mph claim, and the 2000S, which should have allowed a 3s reduction in the acceleration time and an extra 6mph. The two German V6 models (2.0 and 2.3) were said to manage 107 and 114mph, respectively, the 2-litre V6 recording 0-62mph in 12.5s and the 2.3 taking 10.1s for the same sprint. Courtesy of *Autocar* in 1982, we can reflect that the acceleration claims were close to those found by this magazine in independent tests during 1978-79, although the 1600S actually proved more accelerative than expected (12.7s to 60mph), while the 2000S at 10.8s and the 3000S at 8.6s were very close to Ford's computer predictions.

However, top speeds recorded by *Autocar* were well down on Ford hopes at 99mph for the 1600S, 106mph for the 2000S and 116mph for its 3-litre big brother. I am told that the genuine 120mph-plus production Capri is a rarity that has escaped those who measure things accurately. Personally I was convinced of this capability only in the RS2600 and RS3100 that I drove when they belonged to the factory, but under road conditions that are slightly favourable and where you are not trying to launch a car from the MIRA banking (as must *Motor* and *Autocar* for the majority of their tests) I have found that the 1971 uprated Capri V6 and the 3000S were capable of indicating the best part of 130mph. I would not be surprised to find that the RS3100 with its front and rear spoiler and the narrower body was the quickest mass production Capri of all, *if* the owner ensured that the advertised 148bhp was present.

Running changes

When I wrote about the Capri in a large-book format for the first time, many 'experts' assured me the model was dead and

At the lower end of the Capri range in Britain Ford kept shuffling various equipment choices. By 1983, the cheapest model was a 1600L at £4,949, some £4,100 more than the 1969 introductory pricing of the basic 1300! The 1983 range covered seven models including the £5,163 1600LS illustrated here; the 1600 and 2000GL (£5,323 and £5,701, respectively); the 2000S (£6,391); the 2.0 Ghia (£7,341) and the 2.8i to top the British range from £8,125.

would be buried before the book could come out in 1981. Yet Ford personnel always referred in advance to 1983½ as a key date, and so it proved. Still in the pipeline were substantial developments including a five-speed gearbox and fuel injection as well as provision in the schedule for further special editions.

There were a series of minor production and equipment changes prior to the introduction of some meaty performance Capris in the 1980s. The modifications started in September 1978 when the factory began sending through Capris of increased specification following the August holiday shut-down. The L versions incorporated a MW/LW pushbutton radio, while the Ghia's mono radio was joined by a stereo cassette player as a

standard fitment; the S gained the rear foglamps of the Ghia and GL.

In the spring of 1979 there was another equipment shuffle as head restraints, a passenger door mirror and a remote-control external mirror for the driver became part of the GL package. Ghias took on the three-spoke sports wheel, the passenger door mirror and encompassed headlamp washers in their production equipment. The S was allowed a little of the Ghia's additional soundproofing and the driver's door mirror; you can check S soundproofing by merely looking under the bonnet, although additional padding was also inserted between trim and rear body panels.

In April 1980, many of the power and torque figures for the Capri engines were revised for a variety of reasons, such as the use of a viscous-coupled fan on the 1300 and the overhead-camshaft 1600 and 2000 units. The 1300 was rerated at 60bhp, the ordinary 1600 went from 72 to 73bhp and the 1600S to 91bhp at 5,700rpm. The 2000 clambered upwards, too, and instead of the 98bhp that was always quoted for the 2-litre (except in the Escort RS2000, which was always credited with more because it used an electric fan in the Mark 1 and different exhaust manifolding in the 'beak nose' later car), 101bhp was credited at 5,200rpm. The maximum torque figure was lifted from 111lb/ft to 113lb/ft, still at 3,500rpm, and similar slight torque increases were reported by Ford for the smaller in-line fours.

April 1980 also marked the rather more thorough increase in power for the 2.3 V6 of the German-market Capri (plus the UK Granada and Cortina and later Sierra) with 114bhp at 5,300rpm instead of 108bhp at 5,000rpm, mainly due to increased breathing capability through larger inlet and exhaust valves, bigger-bore porting and a compression increase from 8.75 to 9:1.

In January 1981, the 1600S was deleted from the British market in favour of a cheaper 1.6LS with a blend between the 73bhp 'soft' engine and the harder S-suspension, steel wheels with 185 radials and the S-type rear spoiler. The price reduction compared to the previous model was £160. Of course, prices were a primary

The Capri Calypso, seen in the foreground, was one of a series of limited edition variants offered during 1982. Apart from the obvious two-tone paint finish and rear spoiler, the car was equipped with a Capri S dashboard and featured Carla check seat trim. In the background is another limited edition model, the Cameo, with a more basic specification.

Another limited edition model with a sporting theme, the Cabaret featured decorative flashes down the body sides, terminating alongside the rear spoiler. Other features included Ghia door trim, a centre console and a sunroof and, like the Calypso, it was fitted with GL-type wheels.

concern with the comparatively aged Capri in a fashion-conscious area of the market. Just how much times had changed can be gauged from the September 1982 Capri list stretching from £4,949 charged for the 1600L — which replaced the 1300 as the starting point of the range — to over £8,000 for a new top model that had gradually replaced both the 3000S and the 3.0 Ghia, combining many of the Ghia's luxury features with an engine taken from the Granada 2.8i that Ford originally said would not be available in the coupe.

Capri 2.8 injection

Even when the third-generation Capri was first announced to the press, in February 1978, a fuel-injected 2.8-litre Capri had already been built for appraisal, one of many prototypes that had established the worth of combining such V6 power with the extra comfort of Ghia features. At first the exceptionally small volumes achieved by the Capri could be used as a let-out, but gradually the Ford management, influenced by the hard-driving enthusiasm of former Opel/BMW executive Bob Lutz, were persuaded that a Capri 2.8i should be part of their plan to offer genuinely better

drivers' cars to a more technically aware market. Another pertinent factor was that the 3-litre Capri power unit was no longer needed in the rest of the car range and had thus fallen behind in its emission certification for European installation.

Thus, a decade after they had engineered the RS2600, Rod Mansfield, Harry Worrall, Mike Smith and some others from FAVO days set about engineering a 2.8-litre fuel-injected Capri for a 1981 target of 4,000 units. They succeeded beyond anyone's hopes, with a 2.8i competitively priced at £7,995 (or fractionally over £8,000 with the optional duo-colour metallic finish) as it entered the British market in June 1981. Over 25,000 injection Capris would have been made by the time the final 280 version, produced in 1986 and sold in 1987, had gone.

Although a fair amount of engine work was carried out, Ford mainstream management being particularly keen to see that there would be no motor failures under rigorous use, the initial claim of 160bhp at 5,700rpm should perhaps be viewed as an exaggeration, 150bhp being the figure quoted for the same engine in Sierra and Granada models. Ford justified the extra 10bhp on the grounds that the Capri had a dual exhaust system! There was 162lb/ft of torque

The most sporting mass-production Capri of all, on which the 1978 tail-lights and rear spoiler were retained, leaving badgework reading 'Capri 2.8 injection' at the rear and 'injection' on either flank to remind onlookers that those modified Wolfrace alloy wheels are not for decoration only. This sporting Capri is surely destined for classic status.

Interior of a 1983 Capri 2.8 injection for the British market. The flat three-spoke steering wheel remained, along with an instrument layout that was largely unchanged during 14 years of production, though both facia and steering wheel received extra padding to satisfy German safety regulations. Remote-control mirrors, stereo radio/casette players, Recaro seats and a steel tilt-and-slide sunroof were all part of the standard specification.

Ford's rally mechanic and practical engineer par excellence, Mick Jones, kicks up the dust as he wheels the previously pristine Capri 2.8 injection out into the badlands of the Boreham test track!

LVX 902W

at 4,300rpm. It was all enough to provide a genuine 129mph and 0-60mph in a sizzling 7.9s according to *Autocar* figures. Even more important in a fuel-conscious age was the fact that the Bosch K-Jetronic injection allied to the precision of breakerless transistorized ignition provided an overal 21.3mpg even under the duress of energetic testing. At £8,000 the Capri 2.8i proved a road-tester's favourite against such august competition as the svelte Alfa Romeo GTV 2.5 V6 (£10,250) and the BMW 323i (£8,940), both of which had similar overall performance.

The durability modifications made by Mansfield's team to the 60-degree V6 included improved heat treatment for the crankshaft, a larger radiator and thermostat settings which allowed the free flow of water at a lower preset point in order to ensure maximum water circulation. 'In fact, I think we almost carried it too far,' the former Mexico Escort racer told me cheerfully during a tough 2.8i press driving session, which included a few laps of Nurburgring and a speedy motorway trip through France, Belgium and Germany. Rod Mansfield confirmed that a great deal of testing under hot conditions had

failed to show the least sign of overheating under pressure, and we regularly ran the test cars — and my own Capri 2.8i for another 5,000 miles — at speeds up to the 6,100rpm limiter; in top gear this would show as a boggling 140mph, owing to the lying speedometer!

For many critics it was the superb suspension with Bilstein gas dampers, the Goodyear NCT 205/60 low-profile tyres and the adoption of ventilated 9.76in front discs from the Granada that made this Capri so complete. The chosen spring rates of 112lb/in at the front and 140lb/in for the rear (single leaves again) left the Capri firm enough to be enjoyed on a circuit — especially as the diameters of the anti-roll bars had been increased to 24mm at the front and 14mm at the rear. The ride height was supposed to be an inch lower than on a Capri 3-litre but a number of different figures have appeared: 52.2in against 53.2in are the most widely quoted overall height dimensions.

Standard equipment was extremely comprehensive and encompassed considerably modified Wolfrace Sonic alloy wheels (the centre-section depth was increased for Ford), the Recaros

The Zakspeed Capri Turbo was sold through German RS dealers, though not badged as an RS product. The versatility of the basically simple Capri design kept inspiring new variations on the old theme of value-for-money fun, and British Ford dealers were also able to offer a turbocharged 2.8, this time by Turbo Technics, to encourage sales in the last years.

which had been an S-model option trimmed in a soft grey cloth and fitted in a Shark Grey colour-scheme interior that was essentially a combination of S plaid trim insets and Ghia features like the stereo radio/cassette (excellent — I still miss it!) and the tilt/slide steel sunroof (likewise); the sound equipment was the Blaupunkt Coburg model with an FM facility. Other standard equipment included items such as the twin mirrors coded to the body colour (only the driver's had a remote-control adjustment) and carpeting and sound-proofing that could fairly be described as extensive. One small snag was that the large 7J × 13 alloy wheel took up a lot of the shallow boot space when serving as a spare.

Overall the Capri 2.8i was voted by many as the best Capri ever — some said the best Ford — and it put new life into the whole range, along with a lot of respect for its abilities.

Capri Turbo: quickest and rarest

Journalists on the summer 1981 launch of the Capri 2.8i were allowed a glimpse in the Nurburging pits of a new Zakspeed-produced Capri Turbo that would be sold from July 1981 through the German Ford RS dealerships; the price, in September 1982 (when the model ceased production) was the equivalent of £8,893. On paper it sounded very tempting, with 188bhp squeezed from a carburated version of the 2,792cc V6 (normally, this 2.8 gave 135bhp in a Granada) with the help of a 0.38-bar boost from the Kühnle, Kopp and Kausch (KKK) turbocharger. Ford anticipated

that the Capri, complete with glass-fibre wheelarch extensions and a swoopy road translation of the large front and rear wings used on the racing Zakspeed Capri Turbos that had inspired this project, would whistle to 215km/h (134mph) and reach 62mph from rest in just 8s. The Ford Motorsport brochure, with its *Technik, die Spaß macht* (Technology, the fun-maker) motto, records official Capri Turbo fuel consumption as 31.38mpg at a constant 56mph, 25.22mpg at 75mph and 18.96mpg in the Urban cycle.

Talking with senior Ford Motorsport personnel in 1982, and recalling my initial impressions of poor-quality finish, I was assured that sales had been achieved of 'the planned 200 units'. Certainly the panel work finish and spoilers looked as though they belonged on a home-made boy racer and the original engine installation arrangements for the turbocharger were not so hygienic as they later became with a smart crackle finish RS vacuum chamber above the single twin-choke carburettor.

Zakspeed had been producing limited runs of special road cars since 1980 — including some Capris with the glass-fibre wheelarch extensions and a modest 7bhp boost through a new exhaust system — but the Capri Turbo marked a far more ambitious project for the compact production facilities which had been grafted on to the rear of the Niederzissen premises owned and directed by Erich Zakowski.

The V6 engine was carefully developed to give good response rather than peak power, hence the moderate boost allied to the

Only 200 examples of the Zakspeed Capri Turbo were made and sold, so this 130mph-plus performer from 1981-82 is bound to attract collectors. A carburettor-equipped version of the 2.8 engine was used for the simple 188bhp turbocharged conversion.

standard 9.2:1 compression. Over 150bhp, that is to say the power output of a 2.8i or the old RS2600, was developed from 4,000rpm onwards, the power curve rising steeply with 170bhp reported at 4,500rpm and close to 180bhp when 5,000rpm was reached. Maximum power was reached at 5,500rpm with a sharp drop back towards 6,000rpm, while maximum torque was a beefy 206lb/ft at 4,500rpm, but with 144lb/ft or more shown on the engine test data sheets from 2,500 to 6,000rpm.

Other standard equipment complementing the extrovert appearance included either the unique 6.5in rim multi-spoke alloy wheels shown in the brochure or the simple four-spoke FAVO design of 7.5in rim and 13in diameter that was supplied with Phoenix 235/60 VR radials on continental test cars in 1982. At first the Turbos were based on the Capri S, but luckily the wide availability of the 2.8i later allowed Zakspeed to base their conversion on that model, with its ventilated front brake discs and improved suspension. The usual four-speed Capri 3-litre/2.8i gearbox was utilized. A limited-slip differential had always been optionally available for the Turbo at the equivalent price in September 1982 of £226.

The interior of the Turbo seemed almost drab by comparison with the 2.8i, the big difference being the grey finish to Ford RS-branded velour seating that looked somewhat similar to that offered on the Granada injection by Recaro. A four-spoke RS steering wheel, as installed on the Escort RS1600i, looked more promising.

Although I have not driven this turbocharged Capri, I have experienced approximately 200bhp within a straightforward 2.8i, courtesy of AVJ Developments, at Pershore, in Worcestershire. Therefore, I can well imagine that *Auto Hebdo's* comments regarding the brakes of the Turbo when they tested the car ('braking truly not serious') were totally apt! The excellent French weekly found a maximum speed of 217km/h (135mph), slightly more than Ford claimed, but they could get nowhere near the 0-100km/h (62mph) claim, managing only 9.4s. This is not as bad as it sound, however, as they only recorded 10.1s for the 2.8i in the same sprint, whereas most of the British press reported 0-60mph times of 8.5s or thereabouts. Gear speeds with the standard 3.09:1 ratio and the large tyres were: first, 43mph; second, 71mph; and third, 98mph — all taken at 6,000rpm. A fuel consumption of under 18mpg was reported, but most of their test took place on the Nurburgring or in its environs!

Special editions, 1982 to 1986

Capri sales throughout the remainder of the model's production life were propelled by the image generated for the 2.8-litre V6 versions, in Britain at least, but before we explore their glamorous careers as range leaders, let us briefly recap on the contracting four-cylinder Capri range.

The adoption of five speeds for the injection model was announced alongside Cabaret II versions of the 1.6 and 2.0 OHC

In March 1983 the Capri LS began to be fitted as standard with sunroof, uprated S-type suspension, tailgate wash/wipe, revised trim and sportier seating, a more worthwhile package than perhaps its dull name might suggest. It was effectively replaced by the Laser after little more than a year.

The Capri Laser arrived in 1.6 and 2-litre versions, priced at £5,990 and £6,371, in June 1984. External identification was provided by alloy wheels, rear spoiler and side stripes with 'Laser' decal.

Capris in January 1983. Based on the 1600L, the new models were priced at £5,250 and £5,550, not much up on the original May 1982 Cabaret. By March of 1983 the inevitable slimming down of model options had left a basic Capri line-up of: 1600LS, 2000S and 2.8 injection.

The LS had inherited a sunroof, tailgate wash/wipe, and S-type suspension as well as restyled seats and interior trim. The 2000S itself embraced a five-speed gearbox, sunroof, sports seats, opening rear windows and a replacement trim pattern, to become something of a 2-litre highlight at £6,385. By September of that year stereo radio/cassette players had been installed in the four-cylinder Capris and the 2.8i had superior electronic in-car-entertainment.

By June 1984 the UK received the Laser special editions that marked the final run of Capri's lesser cousins in Europe. Like their Calypso, Cameo and Cabaret predecessors, Laser Capris offered a bit more basic equipment in the deal to support the marketing effort

The Aston Martin Tickford Capri 2.8T first appeared at the Motor Show in October 1982. Comprehensive styling modifications and refinishing externally accompanied an engine conversion using a small Japanese IHI turbocharger to produce a claimed 205bhp, resulting in a top speed of 137mph and 0-60mph in 6.7 seconds. The predicted price was £14,000 . . . .

. . . which rose to £14,985 by the time it went on sale, and over 100 were sold by 1987. Later examples lost the plain wheel discs, and the title and badging was simplified to 'Tickford Capri', reflecting Tickford's independence from the Aston Martin car company (itself taken over by Ford!) after 1984.

for a now aged model. Specifically, the Lasers could be identified externally by colour-coded front grille and headlamp surrounds, along with the door mirrors, only the driver's side getting remote-control adjustment.

Standard Laser equipment included some fancy badges, four-spoke alloy wheels with 185/70s, leather to trim the gear-lever knob and a cloth trim called Truro. The full instrument panel was offered, with a rev counter, and there was a quad-speaker stereo radio/cassette with a power aerial.

Lasers were offered with 1.6 SOHC motors of 73.5bhp, or the familiar 2-litre 'Pinto' at 101bhp. The four-speed gearbox was standard on 1.6, but there was a five-speed option and that was standard on 2-litre Lasers.

Ford only claimed 99mph and 0-60mph in 13 seconds for the 1.6, a more ambitious 113mph and 0-60mph in 9.6 seconds for the 2-litre, the latter also available with an automatic transmission that sapped all the the figures save the simulation of Urban mpg (23.7). Laser prices began at £6,175.68 for the 1.6 and escalated to £6,568.52 for the 2-litre.

The S-type suspension was no marketing bull. The front spring

rates went up to 102lb/in and the rears to 114lb/in, whilst the front anti-roll bar was the same 24mm diameter as on the 2.8i. It is possible to fit these items, plus appropriate Armstrong damping rates, to older Capris, but new mounting brackets will be required for the front anti-roll bar of a pre-79 model.

2.8 injection developments

Initial 2.8 injection forecasts were for about 2,500 units annually, rising to 4,000, but my 1983 statistics check showed an average of 5,500 per year. By October 25, 1988, Ford, on behalf of Special Vehicle Engineering, could claim more than 25,000 Capri injection coupes had been sold. That was between June 1981 and the last straggling examples of the 280 in late 1987. The loyal British clientele meant total sales averaged 3,846 per annum over the 6½-year sales life of the 2.8i Capri and sons.

Most, but not all, of the later running and cosmetic changes were directed at the 2.8i, although it is worth noting that the claimed 160bhp of the V6 did not alter in a Capri installation from 1981 to 1986. As noted already, there was a swop over to the five-speed gearbox that was also featured on the Granada of the period. It owed

New look RS-style wheels identified the Capri Injection Special. Grille, bonnet lip extension and headlamp surrounds were colour coded to match the body while the rear spoiler and mirrors remained black. Mechanical specification was that of the five-speed 2.8i.

its existence to the autumn 1982 Sierra SOHC and 2.3-litre V6 models that needed a five-speed fitment initially as an option, later standard equipment.

For the Capri, that five-speed unit (Type N) came in January 1983 and the ratios were: 1st, 3.36; second, 1.81; third, 1.26; fourth, direct 1:1 and fifth, 0.825. The effect was to provide a very much more relaxed motorway mount, the usual 3.09:1 final drive now providing 25.7mph per 1,000rpm in place of less than 22mph per 1,000. It is possible to retro-fit the five-speed to other Capri models. Note that the 2-litre Capris from March 1983 onward (starting with 2000S) were offered in five-speed trim; by 1984 both 1.6 and 2-litre SOHC-powered Capris could be bought with five speeds.

In practical terms a quintet of ratios meant 100mph demanded fractionally under 4,000 revs, and it was only the body's lack of flush glass and retention of guttering that made you realise wind noise was now prominent in comparison with other 1980s motor cars.

That does not mean that the performance remained static. As with so many models approaching old age, Ford or otherwise, extra features meant extra weight and acceleration suffered. Our appendices detail precise performance differences recorded by *Autocar*, but from my own electronically timed work at *Performance Car* I can underline that honest top speeds drooped closer to 125mph and 0-60mph hovered above the 8-second benchmark, rather than the original four-speed Capri 2.8i's 7.9 seconds in skilled hands.

Against that, the standard fitment of an overdrive fifth gear genuinely did improve fuel consumption over the lighter (by, on average, 86lbs) four-speed. Some 1.3mpg was the benefit discovered by *Autocar* and my own experience reported a regular 22-23mpg with the handicap of performance testing removed from our calculations. Official fuel consumption test results showed a slight drop in Urban figures for the five-speed (18.7mpg), but the constant speed 56 and 75mph returns compensated with 38.2 and 30.1mpg respectively.

The next major change for the V6 came in October 1984. At a time when the rest of the Capri range was being 'rationalized', the 2.8i took on a number of useful features and additional showroom temptations that left official kerb weight at 1,190kg/2,623lbs.

It was only a month later (November 30, 1984) that LHD production ceased, but in the meantime £9,500 would buy a 2.8i with a limited-slip differential from ZF, considerable areas of leather trim, attractive seven-spoke RS alloys of 7×13in dimensions and a rather half-hearted attempt at then-fashionable colour coding.

In detail, the leather trimming was applied to the usual Recaro front seat design, edging the squabs, to the steering wheel, gear lever knob and inserts for the door trim panels. The grille, bonnet lip extension and headlamp bezels gained the body colour shade, but the rear spoiler and mirrors remained matt black and the usual 205/60 rubber was retained. For the new look RS wheels were of the same width and diameter as those supplied on previous 2.8i Capris. There was a name change for the brochures to Capri 2.8 Injection

Handsome finale. The Capri 280 came in one colour only, metallic Brooklands green, and colour coding extended to the mirrors this time. 15in wheels were the only mechanical innovation, equipped with lower-profile tyres (195/50VR-15 Pirelli P7s were chosen) so that the rolling radius remained virtually unchanged.

Grey leather trim created an impressive air of luxury in the well-appointed interior of the Capri 280. It was applied to the Recaro front seats, the rear seats, steering wheel rim, gear-lever knob and inserts round the door handles. Plastic parts were colour-matched and contrasting red striping completed the effect. Standard features included the steel sunroof, tinted glass and four-speaker stereo system.

Special, but the injection symbols remained the primary badge on the front wings and hatchback lid.

The 2.8 Specials I have borrowed, or used for illustrations, all came in that plummy red. Yet metallics and two-tone options were listed on what had become a £10,599.08 purchase in the summer of 1986. Sales figures that I obtained from Ford in mid-1989 showed how the Capri became a British buyer's car, and how the 2.8 increased in sales percentage performance. In 1983, of 27,618 sales achieved in Europe, 22,200 were in Britain, so it was no wonder LHD production halted in the winter of 1984. . . . Another key

statistic, often voiced during 1983, was that the 2.8 injection took more than 20% of all Capri registrations in the UK, but by the opening months of 1984 that statistics had slipped to under 18%. It was time for the final twist to the big-engine Capri theme. . .

The rumours had it that a 'killer Capri' with turbocharging and four-wheel disc brakes would see the senior coupe survivor out in a blaze of defiance. There was an element of truth in this, as Turbo Technics were authorized to sell an approved 200bhp installation for the Capri through the Ford network. Yet the rumours probably stemmed from the conversion of a Brooklands Green 280 prototype

Final edition. Just over a thousand Capri 280s were delivered, most of them sold during 1987 and D-registered. It was a fitting swan-song for the model, since the 2.8i on which it was based was widely acclaimed as the best Capri ever.

(C256 HVW) by Ford Special Vehicle Engineering and Turbo Technics.

This Capri, complete with 11.25-inch AP front disc brakes and revised suspension, was registered in November 1985 and was credited with 225bhp and 270lb/ft of torque. In this case the compression had been lowered to 8:1, but the most popular TT kit allied the Garrett AiResearch T3 and a standard 9.2:1 cr. Warranted by a combination of Ford and Car Care Plan, the low-boost conversion had proved reliable on many Sierras and Capris prior to the May 1986 announcement of its availability.

Turbo Technics took the standard 160bhp and quietly turned it into 200bhp at 5,500rpm. Backed by 247lb/ft of torque at 3,800 revs, the TT version of the V6 was a thoroughly likeable enhancement of standard qualities that held the promise of 143mph and 0-60mph in 6.5 seconds. TT recognised that there ought to be chassis changes and optionally offered harder bushes for the suspension and the AP four-piston caliper layout referred to earlier.

Sales of the British turbo Capri were not in the same league as

Geoff Kershaw and his team at Turbo Technics had enjoyed *before* the official Ford announcement. Many potential customers must have been aware that a final edition of the Capri was being readied.

That was the Brooklands Green Capri 280. At £11,999 it carried on many of the mechanical themes found in earlier 2.8 injections, including the limited-slip differential and five-speed gearbox. The V6 remained in official 160bhp trim at 5,700rpm, so the sole significant mechanical change was the inclusion of yet another wheel design, this time the 15in RS alloy. Rim width remained at 7in and the 50% profile of the P7 tyres retained the overall rolling diameter close to that of the 13in with 60-series rubber. Oddly enough, the speedometer relinquished its old inaccuracies and provided a fair representation of true velocity!

The most impressive changes came internally, where grey 'Raven' leather stretched over the Recaro frames at the front and usual +2 folding rear seats. Contrast came from Burgundy red striping, but the grey trim theme extended to the plastics, and to leather for the gear-lever knob and steering wheel rim. Standard

112

Building the last Capris in December 1986. To the right, the fuel-injected V6 is loaded beneath the body complete with ventilated front discs and Bilstein struts, items that had featured in the specification since the first 2.8i. Below, the later Capris shared the versatile Cologne assembly area with the Fiesta (and Scorpio/Granada too). Suitable ceremony attended the completion of the final examples of this much loved model: the official production total has since been revised to just over 1.9 million.

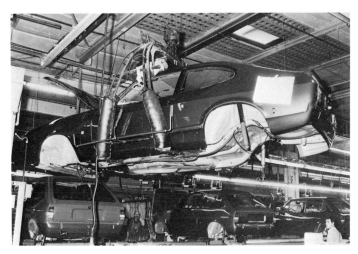

stereo four-speaker system for this model was the three-waveband Ford-branded ESRT 32PS. Features such as the tinted glass and sliding steel sunroof continued from previous injection Capris along with the outstanding ventilation and a dashboard/instrumentation design that must qualify as one of the longest-running in mass-production history.

Externally, the wheels and tyres were joined by unique red and white badges in similarly coloured side stripes, or in the traditional position on the hatchback. No colour options were offered and I am told that the car in the catalogue was actually the Turbo Technics/Ford SVE turbo prototype, a theory supported by the absence of any engine bay picture in that excellent 14-page summary of the Capri's career.

Concours competitors of the future will probably be interested to know that the colour coding went a little further than before, extending to the door mirrors as well as covering the grille and headlamp surrounds, à la 1984 Injection Special. The tailgate spoiler remained in matt, deformable, black, as it had since the 1978 Capri S-types.

Originally a strictly limited final production number was specified and it was though there would be just 500 cars, in green with gold wheels. In fact the orders kept trickling through and Ford built 1,038, including the final press cars which worked their 195/50 VR Pirelli P7 socks off.

The final batch of Capris was scheduled for completion on December 18, 1986 and a small ceremony was held to see a number of 'last Capris' off the Cologne-Niehl line that had contributed so much to the construction of 1,886,647* examples. The last chassi-plate number was WFO-CXX GAE CGG 11896 and it wore the registration D194 UVW in Britain.

For once Ford did retain an historic car themselves (they had to buy back the first Mustang in the USA, *very* expensively!) but the half-dozen last press Capris all got called 'The last Capri', so expect some future claims on that score. In one case I recovered a 'last Capri' that had been broken into twice (D192 UVW), but it was lifted and gutted finally, so the lesson should be learned. Use every anti-theft trick in the book if you want to keep a valuable Capri in London. Like the Cosworth Sierra and some Escorts, they are prime targets for theft.

I think the Capri departed with honour intact (production numbers actually went up in the final year), but I still mourn the fact that Europe's market, slightly bigger in volume than that of the USA, cannot justify fresh sheet metal to clothe a value-for-money rear-drive coupe. Now over to the competition story, one that never seems likely to end, with the announcement of a one-marque British club racing series for the V6 models in 1990. . .

This was the total given at the 'final Capri' ceremony I attended in Cologne during 1986. A 1989 cross-check revealed a slightly higher total, including KD (Knock Down kit) figures. All came from Ford of Britain, Manufacturing department. These later figures are given in the appendices.

CHAPTER 7

Capris in competition

Phase 2: 1978 to 1989

As a competition car, the later Capri received an overall boost through the use of a more slippery body without a weight penalty and the standard fitment of a rear spoiler to S models. The latter was important in the Group 1 production classes (replaced in 1982 by Groups N and A) for the intensive homologation work carried out on the Capri II in 1976-77 resulted in at least 220bhp being put at the disposal of the works-backed privateers in British racing at the beginning of the 1978 season. Therefore, a Capri prepared for the 1978 British Saloon Car Championship had a performance similar to that of some exotic Italian supercars, and hence the rear spoiler had to work for its living, along with the RS3100-type brake discs and the two-piston front calipers that remained in the racing specification from 1976.

However, successful as the latest Capri has been in British competition (Gordon Spice continuing his points dominance of the larger class with the new body, so that the Capri emerged a victor throughout the period 1975-80), the real glamour in the tale of the Capri's competition conquests belongs overseas. Again it was very successful in Group 1 form, even in countries like Australia, where the latest shape has never been sold, and in Belgium, where British-prepared Capris not only took the national title in 1980, but also scored a hat-trick of wins in 1978-80 in the world's premier 24-hour event for saloons, a 'tin-top' version of Le Mans, held at Spa-Francorchamps.

Yet even those 24-hour victories pale beside the German Capri 'III' concoctions for their own championship. I refer to the *Deutsche Rennsport Meisterschaft* which was run in 1978-81 for cars conforming to Group 5, a category which permitted the most radically modified racing saloons and sports cars seen in international competition. In 1982, the series catered for a mixture of old Group 5 cars and the new Group C International Sports Car racing formula, and still the Capri was a star, if sometimes an embarrassing one to its masters, who might well have preferred it not to perform so well in the company of their new Ford C100 sports-racing coupes.

Escort and Capri ancestry

To understand the Zakspeed turbocharged racing Capris, which just happened to wear vestiges of the production Capri such as the front windscreen, side glass shapes, door handles and rear hatchback in order to comply with the Group 5 regulations, you have first to understand that the components beneath those sweeping body lines owed a lot to other Ford competition programmes.

At the start of the Capri programme — during autumn 1977, when Martin Braungart's 1972 successor, Thomas Ammerschläger, began sketching some preliminary ideas — the German Championship was divided simply into two classes. The idea was that Ford and Zakspeed could both learn about the Group 5 Capri in the 2-litre class, away from the all-conquering Porsche 935s of the larger division, and possibly beat old rivals BMW in that 2-litre division to win the title. Thus, from experience with the Escort they had evolved from the old Group 2, they knew that a 1.4-litre turbocharged version of the Cosworth BDA engine with Ford's 1300 'Kent' iron block would give more power than even a full race 2-litre version of the same 16-valve engine. The early appearances of Schnitzer-prepared BMWs with 1.4-litre turbo engines in 1977 had shown that this was the way to

During the 1977-78 winter Ford drew up and wind-tunnel tested a Group 5 German Championship racing version of the Capri to succeed the Zakspeed racing Escorts. Even Ford motor sport engineer Thomas Ammerschläger was surprised how effective the shape proved to be and in 1982 the same principles were to prove themselves against the best Group C sports car opposition.

go in the 2-litre class. Zakspeed themselves ran prototype turbo 1.4-litre BDAs in the Escort prior to the Capri being readied for its debut at the German GP-supporting championship round in July 1978 and realized 370bhp — almost 100bhp more than had been possible from a racing 2-litre!

The heart of the Capri's competition effectiveness lay in the 70kg (154lb) welded aluminium tube frame, which was fabricated by loyal Zakspeed employees Helmut Barth and Bruno Bunk with practical assistance from Zakowski and drawing office input from Ammerschläger. Over this giant rollcage-cum-tubular chassis were laid Kevlar 49 panels, both front and rear wings being detachable via Dzus fasteners. The body was extensively tested in the Aachen wind-tunnel and proved superior to that of the boxy and short Escort in terms of the ultimate Cd that could be extracted, along with enormous downforce on the huge wings. By 1980, Ammerschläger had taken this development so far that a drag factor beneath 0.250 was possible, despite a body over 10in wider than a normal roadgoing Capri. One factor that helped slip the Capri through the air so rapidly was the extensive front spoiler and another was an overall height of just under 45 inches.

The original Zakspeed 1.4-litre Capri turbo made its debut in July 1978, driven by Hans Heyer, when 380bhp was enough to lead its small class rivals. This car was passed on to Harald Ertl in 1979 and was still being raced in 1980 as a 1.4-litre, but with approximately 460bhp.

In 1979 Ford and Zakspeed supported Hans Heyer again in the smaller class, but also experimented with a 1.5-litre version that produced 470bhp and finished third overall in the larger class. Heyer won the 2-litre division in 1979, then went on to win the series outright for Lancia the following year!

In 1979 Ford hired 1978 German Champion Harald Ertl to support Hans Heyer in the small class, the journalist racer [who also appeared in Grand Prix racing with a Hesketh] bringing the Sachs shock absorber sponsorship that had adorned his 1978 Championship BMW 320 turbo. Ertl was killed in a 1982 aeroplane accident.

Klaus Ludwig and the Capri were to prove a Champion combination in Germany. In the 1980 season, when this shot was taken, Klaus won seven rounds, outrunning turbo Porsches, but failed to take the title because points were docked for a rear wing which infringed the regulations. Just visible is the rear end of the ground-effect venturi, a wedge profile tunnel running from the bulkhead to the rear of the car, its downforce lessening the need for that controversial rear wing.

The grille and central badge look pretty standard, but that was about all these extraordinary racers had in common with a road Capri!

Complete with a lightweight aircraft wiring loom and Plexidur side and rear 'glass', the 1978 Capri 1.4-litre Turbo introduced by Hans Heyer weighed 780kg (1,716lb) and offered 380bhp at 9,000rpm. By comparison, the last of the Group 2 RS3100s, with 3.4 litres of Cosworth 24-valve V6 engine, offered some 455bhp in at least 1,040kg (2,288lb). That previous Capri RS3100 programme had supplied many of the basic principles that ensured the Zakspeed turbo was competitive from the start, including the giant four-wheel ventilated disc brakes, the back axle, the front racing struts (although the mounting points were different) and the use of side water and oil radiators mounted in large body scoops in front of the rear wheels. Of course, the details changed over the years, particularly when the power of a later 1.7-litre turbo had to be absorbed from 1980 onwards, and when the authorities banned their larger-engined car from operating with such a large rear wing in early 1980. The answer

to the latter problem was to incorporate a ground-effect venturi stretching from the front firewall to the back panel and screened at the sides by fixed skirts, which made the car a match for the Porsches despite the obvious power deficiency suffered by a 1.8-litre single-turbo four versus a 3.2-litre twin-turbo six.

Engine development was particularly impressive over a period of five racing seasons. The smaller 1,427cc units (actually fractionally under 2-litres when multiplied by the international motorsport factor of 1.4) were giving over 500bhp by the summer of 1980. More than one Grand Prix team considered their use for the 1983 season when Eric Zakowski anticipated that anything up to 600bhp and more could be available in 1.5-litre GP trim. However, Ford would not get involved in further development costs, being more interested in the forthcoming GP engine regulation changes and how they would affect the Ford Cosworth DFV.

In 1981, the last year of Group 5 German Championship racing, Klaus Ludwig finally secured the Capri's first outright Championship victory in the series, running one of three 1.4-litre Zakspeed cars.

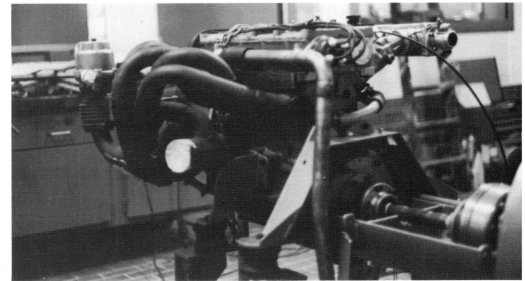

The compact Zakspeed and Schrick-developed Ford Cosworth BDA 16-valve engine on the test bed at Zakspeed's headquarters in 1981. At this time considerable turbocharger development work was going on and there was much talk of a Formula 1 engine, but Zakowski was unable to secure Ford backing for anything other than the Group C sports car programme with the C100 car.

Obsolete? Ford told Zakspeed they would not back the Capris beyond 1982 as the Ford C100 Group C programme had to take priority, but here you see how embarrassingly fast the 1.8-litre version of the Capri could be in Klaus Niedzwiedz' capable hands! At the Zolder German Championship opener on March 21, 1982 the Capri leads Rolf Stommelen's hidden Porsche 936 [just the airbox is visible] and the Group C machines of Harald Grohs [URD C81] and Klaus Ludwig [Ford C100].

The original 1,427cc version with 80mm bore and 71mm stroke eventually gave up to 460bhp at 9,000rpm on 1.5 bar boost from a single KKK 127 turbo and with a 7.2:1 cr. The 1,746cc derivative made ready for 1980 measured 87.4mm by 72.75mm and developed 560bhp with a 7:1 cr and the same boost as the small engine.

The 1.4-litre Zakspeed Capri had won nine out of 14 races in the 2-litre division by the end of 1979, and went on to beat arch rivals like Hans Heyer's mid-engined Lancia Monte Carlo (the 1980 Champion) many times, but it failed to secure Ford an overall national title in the first years. For that they had to wait until 1981, when Klaus Ludwig, who had been German Champion in 1979 when driving a Porsche, defeated Bob Wollek's Kremer Porsche to secure the Zakspeed Capri's first German Championship. Adding to the Zakspeed-Ford alliance's reasons for celebration was a third place in the overall points standings for Manfred Winkelhock in the 1.7-litre version. Winkelhock went on to perform impressively in the 1982 ATS Formula 1 team but died in a Porsche 962 three years later.

In 1982, when Ford made it clear to Zakspeed that they would make this the final year of support for the Capri, the rapid 1.4-litre Capri driver Klaus Niedzwiedz was chosen. The Dortmund resident started the year superbly, beating Bob Wollek's Porsche Jöst 936 turbo sports-racer at Zolder and thrashing both Rolf Stommelen (Kremer Porsche 936) and team-mate Ludwig at the Nurburgring in May. Thereafter, the sports cars got into their

Formula Capri! By 1979 the Ford Capri 3000S ruled the roost in British Championship racing. Here, Gordon Spice, Vince Woodman and the rest of the Capri 3-litre bunch contest the Oulton Park round. Note the flamboyant Dave Brodie in sunglasses on the inside line ahead of the Triplex Dolomites.

stride, but two third places and a second indicated that Niedzwiedz and the Capri were by no means cowed in the face of such opposition. Interestingly, the Zakspeed Capri utilized the Escort RS1700T aluminium cylinder block (a purpose-built block intended for the turbocharged rally car) towards the close of the season. The results were so encouraging that Zakowski devoted much energy in trying to secure fresh supplies, but all the blocks were earmarked for Ford's plan to build 200 examples of the 1700T for homologation, a plan ironically doomed not to reach fruition, though the power unit did re-emerge in the mid-engined RS200.

Recalling the Capri's origins once again was a spin-off from the Zakspeed programme, the construction during 1981-82 of some Mustang-bodied racers which were otherwise to the same specification as the Capri silhouette machines, with only minor dimensional changes. These made their debut at the Nurburgring

in the summer of 1981 and were driven by Ludwig in IMSA races in the USA that season. In 1982 the drivers of these Mustangs included Rick Mears and Kevin Cogan of the Penske team. Zakowski formed a new company in association with Jack Rausch in the Detroit area to service the turbo racers, an activity inspired by former Ford of Germany Competition Manager Michael Kranefuss, who had moved to America in 1980 on his way to becoming Ford's world motor sport boss.

The Zakspeed 'Mustang-Capris' did not reproduce the kind of championship-winning form found in Germany because the American races were much longer, but Klaus Ludwig won their fifth outing of 1981 and qualifying speeds were always spectacular. Perhaps the real value of the German-American alliance was in founding a number of other associated programmes. But Ford personnel never felt Erich Zakowski's heart was fully behind any

Literally in a class of his own. From 1975 to 1980 accessory tycoon Gordon Spice — one of the few drivers to make the successful transition from Minis to rear-drive racers — won the big class of the British Championship. Here is his 1979 CC Racing-prepared 3000S at Mallory Park.

other kind of racing than Formula 1 during the later 1980s. Zakspeed in Germany became BMW-contracted specialists in 1987, running M3s in the national championship.

The production racers

From February 1, 1978 the most recent Capri shape was recognized for international Group 1 competition. At the same time all the modifications that had been allowed for the Capri II and, for that matter, the original Capri were joined by a 7in rim for the four-spoke FAVO wheel, an inch wider than the rims used for the Capri 3-litre. Also recognized early in 1978 was a revised mounting for the front anti-roll bar, which enhanced the Capri's competition behaviour considerably, and the FIA also rubber-

stamped front and rear track dimensions of 56.34in and 56.54in, respectively, a 1.2in stretch in the track over the previous figures owing to the revised rim offsets. By April of the same year, the FIA had been forced to recognize that the varying versions of Capri should have some differences in their racing weights and they listed the first Capri 3000GT at 1,002kg (2,204lb), the Capri II 3000GT at 1,051kg (2,312lb) and the Capri 'III' 3.0S at 1,062kg (2,336lb).

From a competitor's viewpoint in Britain the weight business had little meaning after 1981, when the FIA issued weights at which each capacity class would race. In 1981, the Capri raced in Britain at 1,050kg and received a 1982 boost to its competitive chances against the 3½-litre Rover V8s by a weight reduction to

In 1978 Gordon Spice put Ford back on the Spa-Francorchamps 24-hour roll of honour by scoring the first Capri win since 1972 when he shared his car with Belgium's Teddy Pilette. It was the last race to be held on the classic 8 mile-plus long circuit, and the first win for a Briton in the event since the days when it catered for sports cars. Spice's CC Racing-prepared team also won the 1979 and 1980 events.

Experimentation on induction. Neil Brown's usual Group 1 engine was topped by the triple Weber carburettor kit for the 1979 Tourist Trophy race to run in Group 2 trim.

1,025kg (2,255lb), the BL hatchback being forced to race at a weight 105kg heavier.

The Capri 'III' dominated the overall British race results of 1978-80 and proved very effective in both the Belgian and French Championships, too, many British specialists and several drivers earning a tasty crust from exporting the Ford's winning ways. The 1980 season should not have been so good for the 3-litre V6 as it had to face up to the David Price Racing-prepared Rover 3500 V8s, but the large Rover scored only two victories in its maiden season, one of those coming from 1980 World Champion Alan Jones in a non-championship round. When Tom

Walkinshaw Racing (TWR) took over Rover preparation in 1981 things got tougher, and for the first time since the inception of Group 1 racing in the British Championship a Ford Capri failed to win its class; Walkinshaw himself had won that title for Ford in 1974 and thereafter Gordon Spice had done the job.

In 1982, the Capri staged a remarkable comeback. Spice had left CC Racing's preparation behind him when he set up his own team workshops at Silverstone in 1981. Vince Woodman, the Bristolian Ford dealer whose experience stretched back to Lotus Cortinas and Anglias, had become a CC customer at the Yorkshire Dales establishment in 1979 and switched solely to CC

Vince Woodman took four victories in the 1982 season. Here, he leads the field in the British Grand Prix supporting race at Brands Hatch, but that particular event was a disaster for Woodman; in spite of a scintillating pole-position time he was thoroughly 'Rovered' seconds after this picture was taken. By 1985 he was running an ex-Broadspeed Capri RS in 3.4-litre racing trim to dominate the British national 'Thundersaloons' series.

Capri race preparation from 1981 onwards. Woodman notched up his first win for CC under his usual Esso/VMW Motor patronage at Thruxton on Easter Monday 1981 and carried on into 1982 with such a vengeance that he became by far the most successful Capri runner of the season, scoring four wins to the one recorded by Spice. With one race to go the Capri 3-litre and the TWR Rover 3500 V8 had scored five wins apiece in 1982 and the class title was undecided. After an accident-filled eleventh and

final round Woodman lost the title on a tie-breaker and the Rovers had added another victory . . . but it was the closest Saloon Car Championship racing season seen in Britain.

The major item that had made the Capri competitive once more in 1982 was the free availability of Dunlop cantilever-construction racing tyres which could often be run in a softer and therefore grippier compound than the heavier Rover could handle. A cantilever Dunlop, first tested on a Capri in November

Brian Chatfield, former rallycrosser, kept the Capri faith with a variety of quick 3-litre machines. Here he is on his way to victory at Brands Hatch in March 1989.

1980, offers an immensely rigid sidewall and a tyre tread width distinctly wider than the rim on which it rests; in the Capri's case this means over 8in of rubber on the road and a drop in lap times of a second or more on an average circuit.

The second factor in the Capri equation was an increase in power. Here the British regulations (as in other details) were different to those of International Group 1, so that in the 1980 season a great deal of freedom on induction equipment and freedom to construct racing exhaust manifolding saw the power creep ever upward. Neil Brown, *the* V6 specialist after Racing Services abdicated their throne, reckoned that a good 1979 power output was 230bhp at 6,600rpm. In mid-1980 this was uprated to an average 255bhp at 7,000rpm, with 7,600rpm the maximum rpm allowance (when I drove a 1977 Capri racer the limit was under 7,000rpm). In 1981 the experimentation continued and Woodman had two engine specifications in 1982. I was fortunate

enough to test the milder Weber 42 IDF-carburated example at a soaking Donington and that was also rated at some 255bhp with exceptional torque delivery between 4,000 and 7,000rpm, even moving off from 2,000rpm in the gears with road Capri 3-litre charm and a lot more speed! The ultimate 1982 specification was supplied only to Andy Rouse and Gordon Spice with a third example for Woodman. This could be identified externally by the Weber 48 IDA downdraught carburettor and, as it went past the pits, by the pure formula car wail from the silenced exhaust system coping with 8,000rpm and more! These engines were rated at 265bhp at 7,500rpm and were capable of putting the lighter Capri on terms with its 290bhp Rover V8 adversary. But the lazy 'Essex' V6 engine was never designed to cope with these kind of revs and it was no surprise when Woodman blew up his example comprehensively and the Spice team suffered varying valve gear failures in their 1982 demon motors.

Although Britain stayed with its unique Group '1½' category in 1982, the European Touring Car Championship moved from the old Group 2 into Group A. The same car company kept winning (BMW), but with their 528i rather overshadowed by the TWR Jaguar XJ-S equipe, which took four race wins to the eight of BMW. Competitive Capris appeared only in Germany, where Ari Vatanen shared with Klaus Ludwig a Capri described as Group 1/B. This 3-litre car qualified second-fastest overall, but didn't finish the race and was no pointer to the future as Ford were committed to developing a Group A 2.8i. However, with the strict limitations put on inlet and exhaust fabrication — that they should be standard — the 2.8i proved something of a disappointment when it appeared at the Silverstone Tourist Trophy round in September 1982. Gordon Spice/Andy Rouse shared a hastily converted 3-litre with the Neil Brown-modified 2.8 injection engine installed, along with the rear disc brakes that this category permits. The result was a Capri which struggled to get in the top 10, finishing a humble thirteenth after a troubled run. The frustrating thing was that the well-developed 3-litre had to lose some of its competitive edge with the change in regulations — although even a rear drum-braked version managed to grab fourth place on the last corner of the last lap of this 500km race — and the 2.8i obviously was in desperate need of cylinder heads which did not have the siamese port arrangement that is a production feature.

But Ford were never realistically in a position to extend the Capri's international competition life. German production of LHD Capris halted on November 30, 1984, and the era of the Sierra had arrived. Privateers, though, did not give up easily, and there were a number of worthwhile achievements in the UK that should be recorded. Racing toward retirement, the Capri V6s showed little sign of their age, chalking up three significant results during 1985. Most impressive, from the private owners' viewpoint, was domination and victory in the Willhire 24-hour race at Snetterton, Norfolk. Driven by rodding heroes Roy Eaton, David Oates and John Clark, the 'OK YAH' — number plated Injection led a parade of similar Fords. Through the battering of a hot day and a misty night, Capris not only won, but also grasped third, fourth, fifth and eighth places among the top ten positions!

Also in 1985, British club racer Graham 'Skid' Scarborough won his production racing class with a 2.8i variant, whilst Vince Woodman returned to the Capri fold in a truly spectacular mount. The machine was the ex-Broadspeed RHD Capri RS raced in the 1970s by Dave Matthews (MD at Plaxtons in 1989). Powered by a Swindon Racing version of the 3.4 litre Ford-Cosworth V6 and prepared by Dave Cook (now separated from CC Racing and running his own successful preparation business outside York), the 465bhp Capri pulverized any trace of opposition in the Thundersaloon series, maintaining a perfect 8/8 tally.

Since 1986 and the advent of the Sierra Cosworth, the Capri has been confined mainly to the 'race-your-road-car' championships in Britain. Quite often at club meetings you will see the outline, complete down to the remains of earlier sponsorship liveries, of Capris that raced for Woodman, Spice or Rouse, still mounting desperate attacks upon the plump Rovers, which are often TWR cast-offs. Old saloon car racers never die . . . Talking of which, a feature of my year in 1989 was to examine and value a couple of famous racing Capris, for which substantial sums were being asked, so the chances are that at least some of the legends will be preserved outside the ravages of weekend club racing.

One does not normally link the Capri and rallying in the same successful way as with racing, but 1985 also saw Jeremy Easson win the BTRDA Rally Championship Production category. The next year Easson — who was winning Group N events in a loaned Sapphire Cosworth by 1989 — also finished 32nd on the 1986 Lombard RAC Rally.

Even during the 1989 premier Open Rally Championship series I found evidence that some Capri loyalists were continuing to find affordable fun at the wheel of a 2.8 injection. For the 1989 Circuit of Ireland, Terry Hayward and Gill Cotton revived the Capri that served them so briefly on the 1988 RAC, finishing an encouraging 28th out of 50 finishers in the largely self-prepared Group A 2.8i. I have a feeling that the last Capri competition appearance is still a long way away.

CHAPTER 8

Buying a Capri today

The choice; spares; road impressions

At the turn of the decade, three years after production of the car finally ceased, a pattern to Capri ownership has emerged. The two main groups are the concours fanatics, fast running out of new parts stocks to keep their 1969-78 Capris pristine, and those of varying keeness who keep their Capris mobile for everyday use. These vary from the late Mark 3 serviced by a local dealer to the cheap banger category. Additionally, because the Capri has always attracted a performance/custom following, there are some radically modified examples about in terms of both bodywork and running gear.

Now it is evident that shortages of the most mundane items of trim and body fittings are emerging for owners of the 1969-78 Capri and Capri II models. Major running gear components – engine, transmission and suspension parts – are almost easy to obtain by comparison. If you cannot locate a donor vehicle for trim and body fittings (from door locks to bumpers and panels), forget any plans for a thorough restoration.

No longer can you just nip to the scrapyard and find piles of Capri components, but some specialists do offer help at inevitably increasing prices. Unfortunately the limited run of Capris that interest enthusiasts means that the kind of services offered to Escort owners, like replacement inner wings manufactured to special order, are unlikely to be offered to potential Capri restorers. For example there were only 248 RS3100 Capris made in series at Halewood according to Ford and SMM&T figures. 'Perhaps 50 to 75 of them are in running condition' for 1990 in the opinion of Ford AVO Owners Club Capri RS3100 registrar and Ford RS parts dealership professional Dennis Sellars.

Ford themselves have long since ceased supplying items as varied as complete bodies for the first two series of Capris, or tail lights for the earlier models. However, New Ford Spares in Chorley do have some useful stock left and I have included a list of spares sources, 1989 contact names, plus the Capri Club addresses that will help the determined Capri operator into the 1990s. I also think the old cliche 'where there's a will there's a way' should not be forgotten, adding that constant visits to scrapyards and autojumbles, plus a sharp eye out for dumped Capris, will eventually produce 'the car you always promised yourself'.

The real collectors' pieces among the Mark 1s are of course the RS3100 in Britain and the RS2600 in Germany. Among later cars, the potential of the final 280 series, at only 1,038 examples, is worth monitoring. A valuable collector's car has not emerged from the Capri II range – a good thing for those who like value-for-money coupe-style motoring – because of the absence of homologation specials like the short-run RS versions. Already the Mark 3 injection Capris of 1981-86 are attracting a following beyond the 'Kerbside Motors' level. I expect the first and last (2.8i four-speed and 280 final edition) particularly to be recognised for their merits longer term into the 1990s.

Quoting second-hand prices is always problematical because of the 'instantly out-of-date' factor, but I thought it might be useful and interesting to survey the market in late-1989 if only to give some indication of *relative* values. I found that the bulk of Capri derivatives could be bought in taxed and MOT-tested condition for between £500 and £5,000. The lower figure, and I saw some for less than £500, usually applied to a four-cylinder Mark 1 series Capri. Between £900 and £2,000 took you into the 3-litre derivatives, an above-average V-plate 3.0S being priced at £1,300 complete with five-speed gearbox and Bilsteins in the March 1989 classifieds of the

This immaculate, apparently original and obviously cherished 1600GT caught my eye at a *Fast Ford* magazine day nearly twenty years after its first registration.

Capri Club International magazine. The 3000GXL or 3000GT is a useful source of spares for the RS3100 owner (or those who would fake the RS Capri!) and these tended to attract bids up to £1,800 in good order.

In the £2,000 to £3,000 bracket I found a diversity such as a 2.8i conversion with a five-speed box on a V-plate at £2,000 exactly, or a 1983 2-litre Cabaret on offer for £2,795 with Alleycat wide steel wheels and a sunroof. Those all came from the Capri magazine, but skilled operators will rely on local trade specialists, *Exchange and Mart* (lots of choice, but lots of disappointments in my experience) and – especially for performace derivatives of any Ford – *Motoring News*.

That weekly newspaper underlined that you need over £3,000 to start thinking about the 2.8i in the 1990s, although there was a Group N Capri 2.8i rally car for disposal at £2,995 in July 1989. More typical were prices around £3,500-3,600 to purchase early examples with four-speed gearboxes. Remember that standard equipment for a 2.8i always included a stereo, sliding steel sunroof and 7J x 13in Wolfrace-pattern alloys: they were reworked with thicker centres over the original design that was also popularized on

the MG Metro. Therefore do not fall for the common line of 'all the extras, including alloys, tints, etc'.

The C and B-registered five-speeders I saw were all comfortably over £4,000 and heading for £5,000-plus. A good example was a B-plate Injection Special at £4,800 with 39,000 miles recorded. Expect a 1986-onward 2.8 Special to command over £5,000, especially a sub-20,000 miler such as I saw for £5,695.

Over £5,000 at the time of writing were the cleanest Injection Specials, whilst the 280 final edition from (generally) 1987 registration looked to be in Tickford territory, i.e. not much under £10,000. I have seen Tickfords (which are rarer than the genuine road registered RS1800s, with just 100 made) at £7,950 for a 57,000 miler, but in 1989 they generally exceeded £10,000. Only a special reason, or registration, then took a 280 beyond £11,000. In my view, it will take a long time before inflation means the 280 is worth more than the original asking price of £11,999.

If there is any justice, a proper RS3100 (which will mean one authenticated by the relevant owners club) should be worth more, but there is a long way to go yet. I saw RS3100 examples regularly (difficult to restore) between £2,500 and £3,000 during 1989. To avoid the imitations, my advice would be to contact Dennis Sellars (Quicks of Manchester, RS Department) because nobody has more firsthand experience of the cars, and it would be nice if you repaid the favour by also joining the Ford AVO Owners Club.

Since the RS3100 is the most historically interesting and highest performance standard Capri prior to the injection models (and not a lot slower than many injection 2.8s in later five-speed, plush equipment trim), let us listen to Dennis Sellars on the subject in a 1989 interview we did at a Ford Dunton Open Day.

'The demand we get has mainly increased as a result of the publicity achieved by Phil Boote for his restored ex-Ford RS3100 (RPU 654M), but that interest has increased prices of 3-litres like the GXL and GT because of their obvious spares use to an RS3100 owner. I've registered 135 genuine RS3100s for the Ford AVO club, of which 26 were ex-Ford vehicles; it should also be remembered that (depending who you talk to!) between 50 and 75 were shipped to Australia, and we have some of those registered too.

'If we had talked five years ago I'd have said all that old stuff about getting what you couldn't get from Ford at the local scrappy, but we're beyond that now for the Concours people. Sure, you can keep any Capri going, RS3100 or otherwise, because the mechanical spares situation is generally good, but when you start talking about new parts for bodies, lighting, trim and fittings, future supplies look grim.

'Ford haven't supplied Mark I and II shells for ages and you can judge the trim replacement possibilities from the fact that I have known the company chop supplies in less than two years after manufacture ceases; they just could not keep all those permutations in stock.'

Turning to mechanical specifics, many of which apply to 3-litre models of all ages, Dennis felt, 'You can get most of the running gear new from Ford. Transmissions are not a problem for four-speed Capris up to the 1981 injection, nor after that date for five-speeds. You might get tripped up on a detail, like the Capri II axle being wider than the original series, but the CWP inside is still the usual Ford Atlas and it's just the longer half-shafts and casings that are different from the 1969-74 series. You can get propshafts OK and specialists will look after balancing and replacement joints.

'So far as engines go it's only the 3.1 that is a problem, and we know how to get round that (expensively) now. Assuming the engine is really rough, you *can* save it. You need a set of Powermax +60 thou pistons, then have the block bored; liners at £30 each should be fitted. The liners will be standard size, so they will have to be overbored as well.

'Also expensive, but possible, on a 3.1 is to keep one going that has finished off the front vented discs, parts that are no longer available. The answer is to graft the complete 2.8i front end on because that way you get new struts (which are £100 each anyway), hubs, discs and brake backing plate shields. It will cost over £600 but it's the only way I know to do the job properly since the discs are no longer supplied new,' reported Dennis Sellars.

Whilst we are at the front end, Steve Saxty (writing for *Capri Club International*) highlighted another cure for the front-end shake that affects so many Fords. First advice is always to have the wheels balanced, but if that fails (and it frequently does) have a look into the condition of the front bushes located at either end of the track control arms (TCAs in Fordese). They can soften and deteriorate to the point where the anti-roll bar – which also has to do the TCA location task on a Ford (and many BMWs) – is beginning to shift. If the problem is evident only under braking, then it could simply be warped discs, which I have encountered on far too many hard-driven 2 or 3-litres.

The Capri has always attracted the attention of the customizer; here are two very different examples of the art, both still going strong and keeping their owners happy in the late-1980s.

Ford's X-pack design is still the inspiration for most body-kitted Capris, but watch out for poor quality glassfibre and badly fitting panels on some imitations. Find a good example at a Ford club meeting and ask the owner for his recommendations if you want this kind or result.

Turning to the vexed question of body and trim components, Dennis Sellars applied his knowledge as a former winning concours competitor (his red RS3100 was currently awaiting a major refit when this was written) who has been chasing parts for the public and his own Capris since 1981. 'You can patch and mend to keep a Capri, any Capri on the road, but to keep one to original concours spec is becoming impossible. I reckon there'll be about eight concours RS3100s in Britain by the 1990s and the rest will gradually disappear.'

A gloomy outlook for the rarest production Capri, but what about the largely overlooked big sellers? Our Mr Sellars brightened immediately. Again he knew the problem firsthand because he has run GXL 3-litre Capris when the RS3100 has been absent.

'So long as you don't want an immaculate Capri, things are much better. Body parts can come from a variety of sources, whether Ford depots and dealers, or from the scrapyard. Prices have gone up; I used to get second-hand doors for £50 but now I'm asked £200! You will probably spend most time on looking for the smallest trim items, but on the exterior you will find that items like rear lights are no longer available for the first Capri, nor is a plastic-coated rear bumper for an RS.

'You can get front quarter-bumpers still, but they will often have been damaged, and I have been asked for £50 each. The story on instruments is a bit brighter. The first point is that they are usually reliable. If there is a need to replace the dials on a September 72-December 1986 layout the long production run should give plenty of choice! You will find that both white and orange needles were used in the run,' said this RS parts supremo with an eye for winning detail. Incidentally, the rarest red needle examples are sometimes found in scrapyard 3-litres, and you should remember to find a donor Capri with the same number of cylinders to ensure that the rev-counter is compatible.

In some cases 2.8-litre injection Capris will also be unwitting donors of components to keep older Capris alive, as in the RS3100 front suspension swop already described, so it is often possible to enjoy 1980s standards in a classic 1970s outline. As Capris developed, both 2-litre and 1.6-litre models gradually gained improved suspension. There is endless scope to swop components from older models (particularly the sloppier Capri IIs) and their sogginess for a later layout.

Three different routes to Capri high performance: Phil Boote's sparkling RS3100 (right), a Janspeed turbo-charged 2.8 injection (below) and a Mk 1 car fitted with a supercharger (below right).

Similarly with the five-speed gearbox of the January 1983-December 1986 injection Capris, a transplant for earlier models is perfectly feasible. I am not going to tell you how you go about such a swop in 100 words, but I can say that many Sierras of 1982 onward, Granadas and even later 1.6 and 2.0 SOHC Capris are sources of such boxes. Steve Saxty in the *Capri Club International* magazine did detail exactly what needs to be done (April 1987): back number reprints and membership details from the address given later.

A few Capri owners will want to go the whole hog and fit the V8 engine which that engine bay seems to cry out for. I have now driven both Ford V8 and Rover V8 converted Capris and can only say that the Rover is a much more practical proposition. That is because of low costs in the UK and light weight, which can easily be accommodated by a chassis to the standard of the 2.8i. I would plead for you to try such conversions only on a sound Mark III series, because the body is more likely to be strong enough to take the shock of a 165-250bhp Rover V8. Also, the appropriate suspension and braking steps are most easily taken with the later Capri. If you try and bodge up an old Mark I or Capri II the results could be worthy of a Governmental health warning!

My feelings are much the same if you want to turbocharge a Capri. Ford blessing, and limited marketing effort, was behind both the Turbo Technics and Tickford devices but they were very different ways of applying some 200bhp. The TT Capris were often unmodified from a 2.8i five-speed base and I thought they needed more chassis work (updated front discs, harder bushes at least) before their power could be safely deployed. The Tickford was expensively different and showed a properly engineered chassis,

complete with the back disc brakes the Capri always needed in V6 form.

My suggestion, having driven all the above, plus a few non-TT turbo conversions around 200bhp, is to take a sturdy 2.8i four-speed, and uprate the chassis conscientiously before taking on the Turbo Technics Garrett AiResearch conversions. I am convinced Turbo Technics equipment is the most practical all-round performance-with-docility answer offered to the Ford V6 owner.

For sheer pleasure, regardless of flexibility and practicality, I still have a weakness for a modified, normally aspired 3-litre Capri. Allied to a vented disc brake front end (and rear if you afford it) and uprated chassis with appropriate wheels and tyres, 200bhp and an rpm operating band between 3,500 and 7,000 should stir the adrenalin to addictive levels. Performance? Such a car should dip into the mid sixties for 0-60mph and exceed 135mph, but fuel consumption and reliability are unlikely to match a good turbo or V8 set-up, which is why I am not advocating this 'sprint' road racer specification for practicality!

Mentioning tyres reminds me that this is one of the most debated areas of performance Capri ownership. If you put me in a corner and ask for one brand over all years and models, I would say Goodyear have performed well. I like the NCT for Capris and I understand that the latest Eagle Uni-directional rubber works well. For specific high-power installations I think the fastest lap times on smooth race tracks would come from BF Goodrich R1 or Yokohama 008, but Bridgestone RE 71 is worth assessment for its consistency and wet-weather grip. Pirelli, especially the expensive P7 or P700 series, have featured on X-pack and final series 280 Capris. I feel Pirelli are only at their best when nearly new and that their dislike of standing water is not good news on a car that already struggles for wet road adhesion! Others recommend Dunlop strongly in 205 sizings and I would not quarrel with the Cosworth/ Porsche size 205/50-15 D40 cover on suitable rims for any quick Capri. You can tackle sometimes slippery surfaces with complete predictability: D40 almost writes you a postcard whilst losing grip!

Of the standard Capris that I drove over the years, I must admit that the four-cylinder Pintos (particularly in later S-trim) were much tidier and quicker than has ever been generally realised. I have a sentimental soft spot for the original 1600GT, which introduced me to the model over 37,000 miles in the early 1970s. It handled well after conversion, but acceleration would be described as leisurely in 1990.

Of course the 3-litre and 2.8 V6s were performers and I believe a 300GXL would stand the test of time for affordable fun, whilst the RS models have obvious collectability status. I still prefer the fuel injection RS2600 to the right-hand-drive carburated 3100, but I have to acknowledge that the practicalities of ownership still deter even those with mechanical knowledge and contacts from acquiring them in Britain. I should also say that many of the examples offered in Germany (*auto motor und sport* fortnightly magazine is a good guide) are heavily modified with racing bodywork of varying quality. So the RS3100 is the final objective for British Capri fanatics. Yet, I think many have overlooked the merits of any 1969-71 original series Capri in the cleanest and most standard condition attainable. There are very few such cars about, and you get a whiff of period motoring at the same time.

Whatever your choice, put it through all the usual second-hand purchase tests (pay the best mechanic you can find for the day if you are not qualified to judge mechanical fitness), check it is not stolen or subject to outstanding HP and be particularly cynical about crash or rust damage. Assume the worst and remember that, pre-1978, body condition is all-important because the panel and trim spares position is so poor.

However, since nearly two million were made, you should not be starved for choice. You can expect to be driving one of the most accessible and affordable, cult cars of the 1990s . . . Happy Capri motoring!

Useful addresses

Capri Club International, Field House, Redditch, Worcestershire, B98 OAN.

Cars and Car Conversions magazine, Technical Queries Department, Link House, Dingwall Avenue, Croydon, Surrey, CR9 2TA.

Classic Components, Keighley, Yorkshire.

Dave Cook Racing, Unit 1a, Sheriff Hutton Trading Estate, Sheriff Hutton, York, YO6 5AB.
Tel: 03477 422. (*Race preparation, disc brake rear axles.*)

Ford AVO Owners Club, Martyn Castick (Chairman), 175 Market Street, Tottington, Bury, Lancashire, BL8 3LT.
Tel: 020 488 4917. (*RS3100 and RS2600 only.*)

Ford New Spares, Abbey Mill, Abbey Village, Chorley, Lancashire, PR6 8DN.
Tel: 0254 830343. Fax: 0254 839240.

KT Ford (Spares: Jeff Mann), The Brent, Dartford, Kent, DA3 6DQ.
Tel: 0322 22171.

RS Autos (Chris Nuttall, Simon Clayton), Furness Vale Industrial Estate, Stockport, Cheshire. (*Restoration specialists.*)

Quicks of Manchester (RS parts depts, Dennis Sellars), Manchester.
Tel: 061 865 1621.

Withers of Winsford (rare spares: Cal Withers), Wharton House, Wharton Road, Winsford, Cheshire.
Tel: 0606 594422. Mobile: 0860 611431. Fax: 0606 594422.

Technical data for Capri range

ENGINES, 1969 – 1973
UK Capri range

Model	Engine	Bore × stroke	Capacity	Compression	Horsepower (DIN)	Max torque (DIN)
1300	OHV in-line 4	80.9mm × 62.9mm	1,298cc	9:1	52 at 5,000rpm	67lb/ft at 3,000rpm
1300GT	OHV in-line 4	80.9mm × 62.9mm	1,298cc	9.2:1	72 at 6,000rpm	68lb/ft at 4,000rpm
1600	OHV in-line 4	80.9mm × 77.6mm	1,599cc	9:1	64 at 4,800rpm	78lb/ft at 2,500rpm
1600GT	OHV in-line 4	80.9mm × 77.6mm	1,599cc	9.2:1	86 at 5,500rpm	92lb/ft at 4,000rpm
2000GT	OHV V4	93.6mm × 72.4mm	1,996cc	8.9:1	93 at 5,500rpm	103lb/ft at 3,600rpm
3000GT	OHV V6	93.6mm × 72.4mm	2,994cc	8.9:1	128 at 4,750rpm	193lb/ft (SAE) at 3,000rpm

German Capri range

Model	Engine	Bore × stroke	Capacity	Compression	Horsepower (DIN)	Max torque (DIN)
1300	OHV V4	84mm × 58.8mm	1,288cc	8.2:1	50 at 5,000rpm	68.7lb/ft at 2,500rpm
1500	OHV V4	90mm × 58.8mm	1,488cc	8:1	60 at 4,800rpm	82.5lb/ft at 2,400rpm
1700GT	OHV V4	90mm × 66.8mm	1,688cc	9:1	75 at 5,000rpm	94lb/ft at 2,500rpm
2000	OHV V6	84mm × 60.1mm	1,999cc	8:1	85 at 5,000rpm	109lb/ft at 3,000rpm
2000R	OHV V6	84mm × 60.1mm	1,999cc	9:1	90 at 5,000rpm	114lb/ft at 3,000rpm
2300GT	OHV V6	90mm × 60.1mm	2,294cc	9:1	108 at 5,100rpm	134lb/ft at 3,000rpm
2300GT/RS	OHV V6	90mm × 60.1mm	2,294cc	9:1	125 at 5,600rpm	135lb/ft at 3,500rpm

September 1970: Deletion of more powerful 2.3 for 2.6-litre listed below

Model	Engine	Bore × stroke	Capacity	Compression	Horsepower (DIN)	Max torque (DIN)
2600GT	OHV V6	90mm × 66.8mm	2,520cc	9:1	125bhp —	148lb/ft at 3,000rpm

ENGINES, 1974 – 1978 (Capri II)

Model	Engine	Bore × stroke	Capacity	Compression	Horsepower (DIN)	Max torque (DIN)
1300	OHV in-line 4	80.9mm × 62.9mm	1,298cc	9.2:1	57bhp at 5,500rpm	67lb/ft at 3,000rpm
1600	SOHC in-line 4	87.7mm × 66mm	1,593cc	9.2:1	72bhp at 5,200rpm	88lb/ft at 2,700rpm
1600GT	SOHC in-line 4	87.7mm × 66mm	1,593cc	9.2:1	88bhp at 5,700rpm	92lb/ft at 4,000rpm
2000GT/Ghia	SOHC in-line 4	90.8mm × 76.9mm	1,993cc	9.2:1	98bhp at 5,200rpm	111lb/ft at 3,500rpm
3000GT/Ghia	OHV V6	93.7mm × 72.4mm	2,994cc	9:1	138bhp at 5,000rpm	174lb/ft at 3,000rpm

German engine line as for Britain, except 2-litre SOHC, and opting for 108bhp 2300GT instead.

ENGINES, 1978 – 1986 (Capri III)

Engine range for revised-shape Capri introduced in 1978 initially as for preceding model. 1981: 3-litre V6 replaced by 2.8 injection. 1981: Zakspeed Capri Turbo for German market.

Model	Engine	Bore × stroke	Capacity	Compression	Horsepower (DIN)	Max torque (DIN)
2.8i	OHV V6	93mm × 68.5mm	2,792cc	9.2:1	150bhp at 5,700rpm	162lb/ft at 4,300rpm
Turbo (Zakspeed)	OHV V6	93mm × 68.5mm	2,792cc	9.2:1	188bhp at 5,500rpm	206lb/ft at 4,500rpm
2.8 Turbo Technics	OHV V6	93mm × 68.5mm	2,792cc	9.2:1	200bhp at 5,500rpm	247lb/ft at 3,800rpm

TRANSMISSION AND CHASSIS, 1969 – 1973

Model	Gearbox	Ratios	Final-drive	Brakes	Wheels/tyres	Weight
1300	4sp-Escort	1st 3.543 2nd 2.396 3rd 1.412 4th 1.00	4.125:1	F/discs 9.5in R/drums 8in × 1.5in	Steel 4.5 × 13in 6.0 — 13in crossplies	880kg/1,936lb
1300GT	4sp-Escort	As above	4.125:1	F/discs 9.625in R/drums 9in × 1.75in	Wheels as above/ 165 — 13in radials	900kg/1,980lb
1600	4sp Escort	As 1300s	3.9:1	As 1300GT	As 1300	900kg/1,980lb
1600GT	4-sp Cortina	1st 2.972 2nd 2.010 3rd 1.397 4th 1.00	3.77:1	As 1300GT	As 1300GT	920kg/2,024lb
2000GT	4-sp Cortina	As 1600GT	3.54/3.44 October 1970/thereafter	As 1300GT	As 1300GT	960kg/2,112lb
3000GT	4-sp Zodiac	1st 3.163 2nd 2.254 3rd 1.412 4th 1.00	3.22:1	F/discs As 1300GT R/drums 9in × 2.25in	Steel 5 × 13in 185 — 13in radials	1,080kg/2,376lb

NB: All 1969 models were available with optional 5in rim width by 13in diameter sculptured sports wheels in steel with 165 radials, except the 3000GT, which had the bigger 185 tyres as standard and would therefore only adopt the styled wheels as an option.

TRANSMISSION AND CHASSIS, 1974 – 1978 (Capri II)

Model	Gearbox	Ratios	Final drive	Brakes	Wheels/tyres	Weight
1300	4sp Cortina 1300/1600	1st 3.58 2nd 2.01 3rd 1.40 4th 1.00	4.125	F/discs 9.5in R/drums 8in	Steel 5 × 13in 165—13 radials	1,010kg/2,227lb
1600	4sp Cortina 1300/1600	As 1300	3.77	F/discs 9.625in R/drums 9in	As 1300	1,040kg/2,293lb
1600GT	4sp Cortina 1300/1600	As 1300	3.75	As 1600	As 1300	1,055kg/2,326lb
2000GT/Ghia	4sp Cortina 2000*	1st 3.65 2nd 1.97 3rd 1.37 4th 1.00	3.44	As 1600	As 1300	1,065kg/2,348lb
3000GT/Ghia	4sp Granada	1st 3.16 2nd 1.94 3rd 1.41 4th 1.00	3.09	F/discs 9.75in R/drums 9in	GT: steel std Ghia: 5.5 × 13in alloy	1,170kg/2,580lb

NB: Pressed-steel wheels 5J × 13in diameter for L, XL and GT. Option on these models was dimensionally identical but sports-styled pressed-steel wheel with 'spokes'. Only Ghia had alloy wheels in 1974, but alloy-wheeled Capri S models introduced in 1976.

TRANSMISSION AND CHASSIS, 1978 – 1986 (Capri III)

Model	Gearbox	Ratios	Final drive	Brakes	Wheels/tyres	Weight
1300	4sp	As Capri II	4.125	As Capri II	As Capri II	1,011kg/2,225lb
1600	4sp Cortina 2000*	As Capri II 2000GT	3.77	As Capri II	As Capri II	1,041kg/2,291lb
1600S	4sp	As 1600	3.75	As Capri II	Alloy 5 × 13in	1,061kg/2,335lb
2000S/Ghia	4sp	As 1600	3.44	As Capri II	Alloy 5 × 13in	1,061kg/2,335lb**
3000S/Ghia	4sp Granada	As Capri II	3.09	As Capri II	Alloy 5.5 × 13in	1,171kg/2,577lb**
2000S/LS/Laser and 1.6S option March 1983 on	5sp Type N	1st 3.65 2nd 1.97 3rd 1.37 4th 1.0 5th 0.82	(2000) 3.44 (1600) 3.77	As Capri II	Alloy 5.5 × 13in	(4sp) 1,130kg (5sp) 1,190kg
2.8 injection	4sp	As Capri II	3.09	F/discs 9.76in vent. R/drums	Alloy 7 × 13in 205/60VR-13, or Alloy 7 × 15 195/50VR-15	1,230kg
2.8 injection January 1983 on	5sp Type N	1st 3.36 2nd 1.81 3rd 1.26 4th 1.0 5th 0.82	3.09			

NB: 1600, 2000S and Ghia optionally available with 5.5in alloy wheels.
*Or Granada 2-litre. **Ghia versions heavier by an unspecified amount.

APPENDIX B

Collector's choice: detail specifications

Capri 3000GT: produced 1969 to 1973 (including 1971-72 3000E)

Basic principles shared with other Capris, but uprated specification included the following:

Engine: Water-cooled iron block and heads, Ford 'Essex' 60° V6, originally in Zodiac trim but with uprated bottom end. Capacity, 2,994cc; bore × stroke, 93.7mm × 74.2mm, compression, 8.9:1. Single twin-choke downdraught Weber 40 DFAV carburettor. Gross power output (SAE), 144bhp at 4,750rpm. Peak torque, 192.5lb/ft at 3,000rpm.

Transmission: Diaphragm-spring single-plate cable-operated clutch, 9.5in diameter plate. Gearbox ratios: 1st, 3.163; 2nd, 2.214; 3rd, 1.412; 4th 1.00. Final drive: 3.22:1.

Suspension: Front, MacPherson struts, double-acting shock absorbers, track control arms and anti-roll bar. Rear, semi-elliptic leaf springs with two radius arms and telescopic double-acting shock absorbers.

Brakes: Front discs, 9.625in diameter. Rear drums, 9 × 2.25in with vacuum servo-assistance.

Wheels and tyres: Steel 5J × 13 wheels with 185—13in radials. Optional styled sports wheels on GT.

Dimensions: Overall length, 169.4in; width, 64.8in; height, 50.2in; front track, 53in; rear track, 52in.

Basic new price: £1,341.

Modifications: October 1971 GT and intro of 3000E provided another 10bhp (DIN) uprated second gear (1.95) and taller final drive ratio (3.09:1). Prices from £1,584.45p (3000GT XL).

Options: XL or XLR packs most common with E designation bringing more equipment. Uprated engine and gearbox probably slightly more powerful than latest units. Steel sunroof and vinyl roof were common on 3000E. Later 3000GXL provided with quad headlamps.

Capri RS2600: produced 1970 to 1974

Sporting Capri and Ford's first European fuel-injected car. Many different specifications during production.

Engine: Water-cooled iron block and cylinder heads, Ford Cologne 60° V6, enlarged from 2600GT. Capacity, 2,673cc; bore × stroke, 90mm × 69mm; compression, 10.5:1. Kugelfischer mechanical fuel-injection engineered by Weslake and FAVO. Peak power output (DIN), 150bhp at 5,800rpm. Peak torque, 165lb/ft at 3,500rpm.

Transmission: Modified mechanical/hydraulic clutch linkage with normal 3-litre 9.5in diameter single plate. Original models had following ratios: 1st,

3.65; 2nd, 1.97; 3rd, 1.37; 4th, 1.00; final drive, 3.22. From October 1971: 1st, 3.16; 2nd, 1.94; 3rd, 1.41; 4th, 1.00; final drive, 3.09.

Suspension: Stiffer gas damping and shorter coil springs for modified front MacPherson struts (negative camber front crossmember) and thicker anti-roll bar. Rear, also gas-damped, single-leaf rear spring, progressive bump stop and anti-roll bar (originally had normal top-mounting axle radius arms, then changed over to rear anti-roll bar with mainstream production).

Wheels and tyres: Original lightweight Minilites superseded by Richard Grant and subsequently FAVO wheels, both 6J × 13. Tyres, 185/70 HR radials.

Brakes: Originally 3-litre/2600GT solid discs (9.6in diam). Sept '73: ventilated 9.75in diameter front discs. Retained 9 × 2.25in self-adjusting rear drums.

Dimensions: Overall as GT, but height 49.72in. Front track, 54.21in; rear track, 53.23in. Weight, from 900kg (1,980lb) to 1,080kg (2,376lb).

Basic price 1972: DM 16,195.

Modifications: Numerous, uprated gearbox most important. 50 original lightweight cars differed in detail, some had carburettors.

Options: Lightweight or road specification at first, gradually developing into genuine road car from 1971. Later models gaudy, correct colours should be silver/blue (1970) with white/blue preferred from 1971.

Capri RS3100: produced 1973 to 1974

Basically a 3000GT Capri with 3000GXL quad lamps, RS2600 suspension and brakes, plus overbored 3.1-litre 'Essex' V6.

Engine: Cast-iron block and heads, 60° V6 with all normal 'Essex' ancillaries, including Weber 38EGAS twin-choke carburettor, but distinguished externally by blue rocker covers. Bore × stroke, 95.19mm × 72.4mm. Capacity, 3,091cc, compression, 9:1. Extra capacity via Ford maximum service tolerance rebore (0.060in), requiring new pistons no longer listed by Ford, but available through specialists.

Transmission: Exactly as for later Mark 1 3-litres with uprated second and 3.09:1 final drive.

Suspension: As for 1973 RS2600 with lowered ride height, Bilstein shock absorbers, negative camber crossmember and single-leaf-per-side suspension of rear axle. 'Director's' slightly softer damper settings specified.

Brakes: As for RS2600 with 9.75in diameter vented front discs and 9in rear drums.

Wheels and tyres: Ford Advanced Vehicle Operations four-spoke alloy, 6J × 13 with 185/70 HR radials.

Dimensions: As for RS2600 with 1,050kg/2,310lb kerb weight.

Basic price: £2,450 (widely discounted owing to fuel crisis and Feb '74 Capri II availability).

Modifications: Some cars counting towards homologation requrement (1,000 pa in Group 2) of widely differing specifications. Initial six prototypes by Ford at Boreham and FAVO followed by Halewood factory production in winter 1973-74.

Options: Limited-slip differential obtainable with wide range of RS parts. Racer had 3.4-litre Cosworth Ford V6, side radiators and five-speed gearbox amongst many competition changes.

Capri 3-litre (3000GT/S/Ghia): produced 1974 to 1981

Although this choice covers two body styles — Capri II and subsequent model — the vehicle remained mechanically similar.

Engine: Ford 'Essex' 90° V6 of the same basic construction as 1969 3000GT. Bore × stroke, 93.7mm × 72.4mm. Capacity, 2994cc, compression 9:1. Carburettor, Weber 38/38 EGAS in last European trim. Maximum power quoted 140bhp, but last figure was 138bhp at 5,000rpm. Peak torque 174lb/ft at 3,000rpm.

Transmission: Cable-activated 9.5in single-plate clutch with ex-Granada four-speed gearbox. Ratios: 1st, 3.16; 2nd, 1.94; 3rd, 1.41; 4th, 1.00. Final drive, 3.09:1.

Suspension: MacPherson struts, coil springs and anti-roll bar. Rear, live axle, half-elliptic multiple-leaf springs, anti-roll bar, gas dampers on back of all Capris from 1978 and on S derivatives from 1976.

Brakes: From Capri II 3-litres gained 9.75in solid discs at front, retaining 9 × 2.25in drums at rear.

Wheels and tyres: Alloy of varying types on Ghia and S, from 5½J × 13 of Ghia in 1974-81 to late-model 3-litre S at 6J × 13. Capri II 3000GT had steel 5½J × 13in; S took alloy in 1976. The 1978 S/Ghia 3-litres had 185/70 HR radials.

Dimensions (1978): Overall length, 172.2in; width, 66.9in; height, 50.7in; wheelbase, 100.9in. Front track, 53.3in; rear track, 54.5in (on 5½J wheels, see text). Kerb weight, 1,171kg/2,577lb.

Basic price (1978): 3.0 Ghia, £5,337; 3000S, £4,327 (Sept '81): Ghia, £8,164.31; 3000S, £6,924.36.

Modifications: S-specification in 1976 Capri II important for improved suspension, gas damping. Rear spoiler and cleaner bodywork with current shape. Bigger front discs, still solid, from 1974 Capri II 3000GT/Ghia.

Options: X-packs introduced late in Capri II run with extended wheelarches and 7½J-plus rim widths, big brakes, RS suspension and better-quality Bilsteins. Also some Ghias 'Special Ordered' with manual transmission and rear spoiler in current series.

Capri 2.8 injection: produced 1981 to 1986

Fuel-injected Granada engine with suitably uprated chassis and extensive standard equipment.

Engine: Ford 'Cologne' Granada injection unit with iron block and heads, Bosch K-Jetronic injection and uprated crankshaft. Water-cooled 60° V6. Bore × stroke, 93mm × 68.5mm. Capacity, 2,792cc; compression 9.2:1. Maximum power, 150bhp at 5,700rpm (originally quoted at 160bhp). Peak torque, 162lb/ft at 4.300rpm.

Transmission: Four-speed (as 3-litre) early, five-speed later.

Suspension: MacPherson-strut front with lower track control arm and 24mm anti-roll bar. Rear, single-leaf spring per side, 14mm anti-roll bar and usual staggered shock absorber arrangement, Bilstein gas damping front and rear. Standard power-assisted steering, 3.3 turns lock to lock.

Brakes: Ventilated 9.76in diameter front discs and normal 9 × 2.25in rear drums.

Wheels and tyres: Alloy 7J × 13 with 205/60VR radials; later changed to 7J × 15 with 195/50VR tyres.

Dimensions: As for 1978 3-litre Capris (Autocar measured a 51in overall height) with 53in front track and 54.5in rear. Kerb weight, 1,190kg (2,620lb) in Autocar test trim, 1,130kg quoted by Ford.

Basic price (UK, June 1981): £7,995.

Options: Duotone and metallic paints, higher level audio, X-packs. For details of later special editions, 2.8 Injection Special and 280, see text.

Capri Turbo: produced 1981 to September 1982

A strange cocktail of 2.8 carburated Granada engine, 2.8i chassis, X-pack arches, unique spoilers and turbocharging. The 200 planned production figure had no motorsport objective, but was to bask in the reflected glory of the immensely successful Zakspeed Turbo Capri racers.

Engine: Ford 'Cologne' 60° V6 with twin-choke Weber carburettor pressurized to a maximum 5.4psi by KKK turbocharger. Bore × stroke, 93mm × 68.5mm. Capacity, 2,792cc, compression, 9.2:1. Maximum power, 188bhp at 5,500rpm. Peak torque, 206lb/ft at 4,500rpm.

Transmission: As for 2.8i.

Suspension: As for 2.8i. Brakes: As for 2.8i.

Wheels and tyres: 6.5 × 13in alloy with 235/60 VR low-profile steel-braced radials.

Dimensions: Overall length, 174.8in; width, 70.07in; no height or track measurements given. Kerb weight, 1,225kg (2,695lb).

Basic price: Equivalent to £7,880 at July 1981 launch in Germany.

Options: 7.5 × 13in alloy wheels; limited-slip differential; metallic paints.

APPENDIX C

Production and sales figures

European Capri production by year

Year	Volume	KD kits
1968	3,855	15
1969	213,979	13,910
1970	238,913	15,800
1971	211,289	6,035
1972	198,875	250
1973	233,325	1,100
1974	183,706	655
1975	100,050	450
1976	101,103	–
1977	91,587	–
1978	69,112	
1979	85,420	
1980	41,755	
1981	34,658	
1982	25,832	
1983	27,618	
1984	19,508	
1985	9,262	
1986	10,710	
Grand total	**1,900,557**	

Note: The official total quoted at the 'final Capri' ceremony in Cologne (1,886,647) did not tally with earlier computer-rounded statistics. This prompted a check with Ford Motor Co Manufacturing Division, UK, in July 1989, resulting in the figures given here which include KD (Knock Down kit) totals not previously available. KD Operations ceased supplies of kits in 1975. Some 337,491 Capris were made at Halewood, Merseyside. In October 1976 all Capri production shifted to Germany. Notes from Ford of Germany indicate that October 31, 1974 saw production of the last Mark 1 Capri. About 124 Capri IIs were preproduction models made in 1973; full production began in January 1974. Some 170 examples of the third-generation Capri were made in 1977 prior to its March 1978 launch.

UK sales analysis 1981-85
In its last years on the market, 1986-87, Capri sales were dominated by the 2.8i specials, but figures for the preceding five years indicate a different and changing balance of popularity between larger and smaller-engined versions.

Year	Total sold	1.3	1.6	2.0	3.0	2.8i
1981	22,289	537	13,264	5,894	1,060	1,434
1982	19,403	52	11,198	4,873	21	3,259
1983	22,254	3	11,399	6,223	–	4,629
1984	16,328	–	8,589	4,341	–	3,998
1985	11,075	–	5,013	3,466	–	2,596

In 1980, Ford sold 31,187 Capris on the UK market, of which 2,265 were the 3-litre model — just over 7.2%. In 1979 they had sold 4,670 3-litre Capris, so demand for that V6 model had slumped to less than half. In 1985, on the other hand, while total Capri sales had shrunk to just over 11,000 units, the percentage of V6s in the form of the 2.8i had risen to more than 23%.

In 1983, five-speed, four-speed and automatic Capris were offered and the company quoted 12,297 as four-speed; 9,957 as five-speed; and 405 as automatics. Calculate that that makes 22,659 cars rather than the sales figures given and note that with Ford, as elsewhere, statistics should always be treated with caution!

APPENDIX D

Chassis identification

A number of code variations have been used during the life of the Ford Capri, but in all cases that I have encountered you will find the vehicle chassis plate (or VIN: Vehicle Identification Number) on the forward transverse rail under the bonnet, normally close to the radiator. So far as I am aware, basics like the opening capital letter B for Britain and G for Germany, the only two countries to manufacture complete cars, have remained unchanged throughout the series. Experts on the parts side inside Ford tell me that so far as ordering spares is concerned the basic system really recognizes no difference between Capri II and its 1978 successor. However, from January 1981 there was a change in identifying the manufacturing source with a series of letters or numbers to open the sequence such as SFA (Ford at Brentwood, GB) and WFO (Ford Werke, Köln), which serves more to identify the company arm responsible for administration rather than the location of the plant. During the Capri's life, mass-production was concentrated on Halewood, in Britain (1968-October 1976), Saarlouis, on the Franco-German borders (1970 onwards for complete cars and some pressings prior to this) and the main Cologne (Köln) Niehl plant (1968 to date). A few Capri RS2600s were made in the pilot plant in Cologne and some of the RS3100 prototypes came from Ford Competitions at Boreham: in both cases we are talking of extremely low numbers, a mere half-a-dozen in the case of the RS3100.

1969-74 Capris

A typical original-series chassis plate might read thus:

BA EC KR 10001

The first letter referred to the country of assembly. For a Capri the opening letter should always be B for Britain or G for Germany.

The second letter refers to the assembly plant. In this fictitious case I have suggested that A for Cologne should follow the Ford of Britain opening! Don't be caught the same way; the B for Britain should be followed by a B for Halewood. For rare reference it should be noted that F stood for Aveley in those days, C for Saarlouis and B in a Ford European context for Genk in Belgium.

Next we have the letters EC which are taken together and simply mean Capri, the E for Capri and C for a coupe body.

Next we listed KR, two letters which would give us not only the year, but also the month of manufacture. As a guide, K = 1970; L = 1971; M = 1972; N = 1973; P = 1974; R = 1975; S = 1976 and T = 1977. Thus you can see that the principle of using a letter to denote the year stayed far beyond the original Capri series and indeed it still has its place today.

In our KR sequence, K was 1970 and R denoted the month. This second letter rotates year by year so that R = February in 1971, but June in 1972, October in 1973, and so on. I have a Capri parts book which lists 84 possible letter and month designations, so you must be content with knowing just the year your car was originally made unless you have access to a Ford dealer's microfilm parts listings, or one of the larger service literature publications.

The five-digit sequence number was always allocated from 1001 to 99999.

Separate boxes provided the following information. Drive: 1 = LHD, 2 = RHD. Next under the heading MOTOR ENGINE on the plate would be two letters signifying capacity in round figures and whether high or low compression. For instance, U meant 2,600cc and Y High Compression. In Britain, the common Capri engine sizes of the period were H = 3000V6; N = 2000V4; X = 1600 High Compression; W = 1600 LC; S = 1300HC; T = 1300LC; and R = 1600GT. In Germany, the equivalent letters beneath the MOTOR ENGINE box were: J = 1300; E = 1500; L = 1600; M = 1700; N = 2000; Y = 2300; U = 2600 and H = 3000.

The eighth box is headed ACHSE AXLE and again works on a lettering principle where 3.22 is indicated by R, 3.09 by L, and so on.

The final box on the 1969-onward Capris was simply headed FARBE COLOUR and here 14 letters of the alphabet and seven numbers were used to identify the factory paint used. For collectors this could be vital, so here are the codes: A = black; B = white; D = grey; E = light blue; G = dark blue; J = light red; M = light green; N = dark red; P = non-standard dark red; T = light yellow; S = metallic gold; Y = non-standard colour order; K = dark yellow and U = non-standard dark blue.

Amongst the numbered colour codes for Capri, the following were designated: 1 = metallic blue; 2 = metallic grey; 3 = metallic silver; 5 = metallic green (light); 6 = metallic green (dark) and 7 = metallic brown.

Capri II to III prior to January 1981

The general principles remained the same, with B for Britain and G for Germany starting the sequence. Next came the plant code. Capri simply became E (third letter in) with C pedantically defined as coupe; the fifth letter carried on the letter and year system. Thus U = 1978; V = 1979; W = 1980; X = 1981 and Y would equal 1982, although the system had officially changed before that could be employed. Again a five-digit serial number was used after the year-and-month lettering.

Capri III from January 1981

From January 1981 a typical Capri plate might look thus:

WFOCXXGAECCU 43267

The five figures at the end remain the serial number, but the opening WFO designated Ford Werke Cologne under a world source of manufacture system that Ford had to adopt. No Capri should have SFA as the opening letters as this identifies Ford at Brentwood. The XX are irrelevant before the previous Capri plate system of country (G = Germany), plant (A = Cologne), car (E = Capri) and body (C = coupe).

Also contained on the plate these days are a total weight, a maximum permissible towing weight in laden state and how the maximum permissible weight is distributed front and rear, all in kilograms. An engine box with R = 2.8 Injection is included, along with plainly listed codes for transmission, axle and trim. These are arranged alongside the main coding, serial number and weight details previously discussed.

The bottom line contains the vehicle type code, which version, colour and any KD information, the latter being irrelevant to us. Note that 1 or A signify LHD, 2 or B = RHD, according to year of build. The Type information begins with G for Germany, EC for Capri Coupe, and has P for 1974 as the year of introduction. Popular Capri colour codes today include: B1 = diamond white; P1 = sunburst red; V1 = stratos silver; C1 = dove grey; while 61 = crystal green. Some Capri injections and limited edition cars came in duotones to complicate the codes further!

Performance figures for sporting Capris

	'Mark 1' series							Capri II series
	1300GT **1,298cc** **64bhp**	**1600GT** **1,599cc** **86bhp**	**1600XL** **1,593cc** **72bhp**	**2000GT** **1,996cc** **92.5bhp**	**3000GT** **2,994cc** **128bhp**	**3000E** **2,994cc** **138bhp**	**3000GXL** **2,994cc** **140bhp**	**1300** **1,298cc** **50bhp**
Maximum mph (best)	93 (94)	96 (98)	98 (100)	106 (107)	113	122	122	86 (88)
0-30mph (secs)	4.3	4.2	3.8	3.5	3.2	3.1	3.0	5.1
0-40mph	6.8	6.4	5.9	5.5	4.9	4.8	4.3	8.3
0-50mph	10.4	9.4	9.0	7.5	7.6	6.5	6.0	12.4
0-60mph	14.8	13.4	12.9	10.6	10.3	8.4	8.3	18.8
0-70mph	21.5	18.4	18.2	14.8	13.8	11.4	11.2	28.0
0-80mph	33.0	27.5	26.0	19.9	18.4	14.7	14.6	46.7
0-90mph	—	44.7	40.6	28.5	24.9	20.2	18.9	—
0-100mph	—	—	—	40.9	34.9	27.5	25.1	—
Standing ¼-mile (secs)	19.5	18.8	18.9	18.2	17.6	16.2	16.6	21.0
30-50mph (4th gear)	12.8	10.0	9.9	9.3	7.2	7.1	7.2	15.8
40-60mph	14.0	10.6	10.5	9.7	6.9	7.0	7.2	16.6
50-70mph	16.4	11.9	12.0	10.9	7.7	7.5	7.5	19.4
60-80mph	21.5	14.7	14.8	12.1	8.9	8.0	8.3	33.9
70-90mph	—	25.8	23.0	14.3	10.3	9.8	9.5	—
80-100mph	—	—	—	20.4	16.7	12.4	11.6	—
Overall mpg	24.3	24.8	27.4	22.0	19.3	21.5	20.7	28.7
Typical mpg	26.0	25.0	30.0	23.0	21.0	24.0	22.0	31.6
Kerb weight (lb)	2,020	2,053	2,121	2,212	2,374	2,430	2,519	2,178
Test published	2/70	2/69	12/72	7/69	10/69	1/72	3/73	4/76

	Capri II series			Capri III series				
	1600GT **1,593cc** **88bhp**	**2000S** **1,993cc** **99bhp**	**3000S** **2,994cc** **138bhp**	**2000S** **1,993cc** **98bhp**	**3000S** **2,994cc** **138bhp**	**2.8i 4sp** **2,792cc** **160bhp**	**2.8i 5sp** **2,792cc** **160bhp**	**Tickford** **Turbo** **205bhp**
Maximum mph (best)	104 (106)	106 (110)	117 (119)	107	118	129	125	137
0-30mph (secs)	3.7	3.3	3.0	3.4	2.9	2.8	2.6	2.5
0-40mph	5.8	4.9	4.6	5.6	4.4	4.2	4.1	3.9
0-50mph	8.1	7.5	6.5	7.8	6.4	6.0	6.1	5.2
0-60mph	11.4	10.4	9.0	10.8	8.6	7.9	8.3	6.7
0-70mph	16.0	14.9	12.2	15.0	11.5	10.7	10.9	8.9
0-80mph	22.0	21.0	16.4	20.2	15.5	13.9	14.9	11.3
0.90mph	34.1	30.1	21.6	30.0	20.0	17.7	19.5	14.3
0-100mph	–	51.1	30.3	45.4	28.1	23.4	26.9	18.2
Standing ¼-mile (secs)	18.2	17.9	17.0	17.7	16.6	16.2	16.3	15.1
30-50mph (4th gear)	13.1	10.6	8.6	–	–	–	–	–
40-60mph	13.1	10.4	8.6	–	–	–	–	–
50-70mph	13.9	11.6	9.2	11.2	7.8	8.2	9.9	5.3
60-80mph	15.5	13.4	10.3	–	–	–	–	–
70-90mph	19.9	16.9	11.7	–	–	–	–	–
80-100	–	30.8	15.1	23.7	12.7	10.6	14.1	6.3
Overall mpg	27.4	24.0	23.1	25.6	19.5	21.3	22.6	21.7
Kerb weight (lb)	2,220	2,273	2,574	2,273	2,646	2,620	2,706	–
Test published	3/74	6/75	11/76	10/79	3/78	6/81	12/84	10/83

All test figures reproduced by kind permission of *Autocar*.